Additional Praise for *Startup Wealth*

"The dirty secret is most entrepreneurs make costly mistakes the first time around. If you're building a successful business, you must read Joyce Franklin's book to make sure your business success translates into maximum personal success and wealth creation."

—**Paul Allen**, founder of Tribe of Angels,
Startup Accelerator Leader, Strategist, and Advisor

"This book contains a wealth of genuinely usable tips and advice, set against a background of entertainingly presented tales of Silicon Valley failure and success. Joyce has compiled a terrific combination of tactical moves informed by factual lessons learned."

—**Lise Buyer**, Principal and Founder, Class V Group

"*Startup Wealth* covers a broad range of topics, from personal finance to tax planning, when working at a startup, whether during the lean years or a liquidity event. The book is also interspersed with relevant anecdotes from entrepreneurs that make it an enjoyable read. Even if you don't end up at the next Facebook, the advice on managing wealth through the startup process is well worth reading."

—**Eric Deal**, Engineer and President, Cyclic Design

D1265145

"Good ideas—defining the steps to startup success, for example—are not hard to find; business how-to books are full of them. What's scarce is persuasive evidence that these ideas really work, particularly when they seem to challenge conventional wisdom. Joyce Franklin's *Startup Wealth* documents her entrepreneurial prescriptions with tips and profiles drawn from interviews with more than 65 tech founders and CEOs. The lessons she offers aren't "textbook"; rather, they derive from the experiences of men and women whose career paths illustrate the "Entrepreneur's Wheel of Life" that Franklin describes. There's no shortcut to success, but *Startup Wealth* offers real-world guidance that's proved its value."

—Stevenson Hawkey, PhD, Director of the Financial Planning Program, Department of Finance and Economics, Golden Gate University

"While many books have been written about entrepreneurism, few ever address the important intersection between the financial success of the company and the personal financial success of the entrepreneur. In this book, Joyce Franklin provides an excellent guide on how to balance between the two, replete with valuable stories of entrepreneurs who have already been down this path and are willing to share their successes and failures. Whether you're an entrepreneur trying to navigate your own balance between business and personal financial success, or an advisor working with entrepreneurs, you should find the stories and knowledge that Franklin shares to be of enormous value!"

—Michael E. Kitces, CFP®, CLU, ChFC
Publisher, *The Kitces Report* & *Nerd's Eye View*
Partner, Director of Research, Pinnacle Advisory Group

"This book should be required reading for all entrepreneurs. Stories abound of entrepreneurs who lost it all due to poor planning after a liquidity event. *Startup Wealth* includes practical tips and entertaining, real-life case studies to illustrate how to protect the wealth created from monetizing years of hard work on the Entrepreneur's Wheel of Life."

—Tanya Shaw Steinhofer, CFA,
Former President, Financial Planning Association of San Francisco

Dr. TM —
Thanks and Best wishes,
Joyce

6/27/16

Startup Wealth

The Entrepreneur's Guide
to Personal Financial Success
and Long-Term Security

Joyce L. Franklin, CPA, CFP®
Rubydon Press

Publisher's Cataloging-In-Publication Data

Franklin, Joyce L.

Startup wealth : the entrepreneur's guide to personal financial success and long-term security / Joyce L. Franklin, CPA, CFP.

pages : illustrations ; cm

Issued also as an ebook.

Includes bibliographical references and index.

ISBN: 978-0-9916172-2-7

1. New business enterprises--Finance. 2. Businesspeople--Finance, Personal. 3. Entrepreneurship. 4. Success in business. I. Title.

HG4027.6 .F73 2014

658.15/224

For permission to reprint, and for bulk order information, contact Info@RubydonPress.com.

Cover design by Randle Design.
Interior design by Ponderosa Pine Design, Vicky Vaughn Shea

RUBYDON PRESS
Larkspur, CA

To my clients, and to all entrepreneurs.

CONTENTS

INTERVIEWEES

Samuel N. Adler
Director of Global Demand Generation, Zuora, Inc.

John Bowen
CEO, Financial Advisor Select, LLC
CEO, CEG Worldwide LLC

David Buchanan
Former Manager of Asia Pacific, Extreme Networks

Roy Bukstein
CFO, MMM Management
Former CFO, Oracle

Lise Buyer
Principal and Founder, Class V Group

Ed Callan
Owner, Callan Consulting
Project Faculty, Wharton Global Consulting Practicum

Jonathan Cardella
CEO, NeighborCity®
Former CEO, OTravel.com, Inc., D/B/A Overstock.com Travel

Robert M. Carter
Principal, RMC Development
Former SVP of Content and Business Development, NuvoMedia, Inc.

Mitch Cohen
Former Managing Director, Hellman & Friedman LLC

Stephanie Coutu
Partner, Arnold & Porter LLP

Edward Deibert
Partner, Arnold & Porter LLP

Lara Druyan
Founding Partner, G&B Partners
Vice Chairman of the Board of Trustees, City of San Jose Retirement System

Martin Eberhard
Founder and Former CEO, Tesla Motors Inc.

Leland Fong
Former Senior Network Architect/Project Manager, Inovant (a subsidiary of Visa Inc.)

Eliot Franklin
Principal Engineer, Entropic Communications

Mark E. Galant
CEO, Tydall Trading
Founder, GAIN Capital

Rachel Garb
Designer & Manager, Google

Eric Gold
Sales Director, Couchbase

Ken Goldman
CFO, Yahoo!
Former CFO, Fortinet (during the IPO)
Former CFO, Siebel Systems
Former CFO, Excite@Home Network (during the IPO)

Jason Graham
Managing Director, WTAS

Peter Herz
CEO, WUCO Capital, LLC
Co-Founder and Former CEO, 3ware

Michael Irvine
Partner, Gunderson Dettmer

Darrell Kong
Former Director of Venture Capital Services, Fenwick and West

Jim Koshland
Partner, DLA Piper

Danny Krebs
Partner, Alliance Counsel LLP

Jamis MacNiven
Owner, Buck's of Woodside

Dee Anna McPherson
Vice President of Marketing, HootSuite

Lesa Mitchell
Vice President of Innovation & Networks, Ewing Marion Kauffman Foundation

Marlee Myers
Managing Partner, Pittsburgh Office of Morgan, Lewis & Bockius LLP

Rob Nail
CEO & Associate Founder, Singularity University
Co-Founder and Former CEO, Velocity11

Lee Pantuso
CFO, NeoCarta Ventures
CFO, CMEA Capital

Sonja Hoel Perkins
Managing Director, Menlo Ventures

Richard Pivnicka
Honorary Consul General, Czech Republic
Member of the Board of Directors, Gerson Bakar & Associates
Former VP and General Counsel, Gerson Bakar & Associates

Joe Preis
CEO, Longitude Properties, Inc.
Former CEO, MetroRent

Brendan Richardson
Co-Director, Galant Center for Entrepreneurship, McIntire School Foundation
at the University of Virginia
General Partner, Northface Ventures

Laura Roden
Founder, Capital Formation Consultants, LLC
Former President & CEO, Silicon Valley Association of Startup Entrepreneurs
(SVASE), now known as SVForum

Stephen Roth
CEO, Carmel Software Corporation

Jeff Russakow
CEO, Findly
Former Executive VP and Chief Customer Officer, Yahoo!

Alexandra Derby Salkin
Vice President for Philanthropic Services, Marin Community Foundation

Santosh Sharan
VP of Product Management & Strategy, ZoomInfo
Founder and Former CEO, Keisense, Inc.

Tiffany Shlain
Founder and Director, Moxie Institute Film Studio + Lab
Founder, The Webby Awards

David Spark
Founder, Spark Media Solutions, LLC

David Stern
CFO, Greenberg Brand Strategy

Marc Tarpenning
Founder and Former VP Electrical Engineering, Tesla Motors Inc.

Nicolai Wadstrom
Founder, BootstrapLabs

Rebecca Weeks Watson
VP of Business Development, RadiumOne, Inc.

Bill Weihl
Manager of Energy Efficiency and Sustainability, Facebook

Mark Cameron White
Partner, White Summers Caffee & James LLP

Bruce Wilford
MTS, Graphite Systems, Inc.
Former Distinguished Engineer, Cisco

Sylvia Yam
VP of Business Development, Sincerely
Former Director of Business Development, Tiny Prints, Inc. and Shutterfly

Some interviews were conducted in confidentiality, and the names of those interviewees are withheld by mutual agreement.

PREFACE

WHAT IS THE BEST WAY TO MAXIMIZE AND PRESERVE financial success in the complex and dynamic world of startups and sudden liquidity events? And what is the nature of the creative energy that drives entrepreneurs?

To answer these questions and more, I conducted more than 65 interviews with leading high-tech entrepreneurs, executives, and notables. My findings—along with my own observations—are in this book. Its contents are based on the Entrepreneur's Wheel of Life (see chart on page 9), a graphical representation of the common patterns discovered through my research.

The book begins with an analysis of what happens in the early days of a startup in Phase 1 and describes the ramp-up to a liquidity event in Phase 2. A brief chapter on liquidity events (defined as an IPO, merger, or sale) follows. Finally, I address the many possibilities in the post-event period, Phase 3. After Phase 3, most entrepreneurs return to Phase 1 and start another company, which sets them apart from their employees, who may retire after a single significant liquidity event. Sprinkled throughout the book are tax and financial planning tips, and, if you're short on time, I've included helpful checklists at the end of each chapter for quick reference.

Completing a cycle around the Entrepreneur's Wheel of Life usually means the fulfillment of a lifelong goal: creating and building a company, then monetizing your efforts. It could include unprecedented wealth, which brings with it new responsibilities and challenges. In my comprehensive guide to each phase, you'll learn how to create and hold on to tangible wealth from your dedicated execution of big ideas.

At this point, you may be wondering why a CERTIFIED FINANCIAL PLANNER™ would write an entire book specifically dedicated to the personal finances of entrepreneurs, and what new insights I could bring to the table. Knowing my story will help answer these questions.

I am, in my heart, an entrepreneur. After earning a business degree from the University of Virginia, I started a punkish Washington, D.C., nightclub in the late '80s. This was a creative venture, and my business savvy helped it thrive. Running a club was exciting, and I loved the entertainment world. But as I grew and matured, the nightclubbing scene became stale for me, and I craved a career with a more lasting impact on the greater good. So I left the creative world and went back to my left-brain roots. I became a CPA.

But I didn't stay away from the entrepreneurial world for long. Over 25 years, I have created a handful of companies, including my current and favorite venture, in which I get to help families achieve their financial and life goals every day. However, my experience building and running a variety of businesses is just one reason for my interest and unique expertise in the personal finances of entrepreneurs.

My husband is also an entrepreneur. He built a successful high-tech business and sold it to software maker Autodesk in 2008 (see page 106 for the story of his liquidity event). His experiences have enlightened me about the emotional side of a liquidity event firsthand—including the excitement, negotiation, realization that it might not happen, and finally the completion of the deal.

My husband's experience drove home to me that not everyone understands the value of financial planning—a lesson I first learned from my own parents, who were not planners. They were born during the Great Depression, and like so many members of "The Greatest Generation," its lasting scars made them fearful of money. They prized education and art, and made a lifestyle choice to pursue aesthetics and learning over asset accumulation.

Like most people, I learned from my parents' failures, as well as their successes. Their fears and apathy about taking charge of their financial health ultimately worked to my advantage and sparked my fascination. I realized that a fusion of my creativity, confidence, and knowledge in the financial planning arena could be the perfect way to bring unparalleled freedom to many.

What they may have lacked in financial acumen, my parents made up for by teaching me early on that enjoying life was the key to happiness. It became obvious to me that to have the lifestyle you want, you need to make smart decisions about money. While people in the tech community give their lives to their companies, they often don't recognize the full upside of their dedication because they fail to plan for their personal financial security. Knowing the entrepreneurial patterns of building a company, the tax rules around equity awards and elections, and the traps so many fall into can help you to preserve your wealth.

The simple truth is that wealth gives us choices. To that end, I'm here to help entrepreneurs and others in the tech community with their most important goals: preserving wealth, taking care of family, mitigating income taxes, and protecting assets. Smart wealth planning can ensure the best possible future for you and your loved ones.

This is my passion.

Joyce L. Franklin, CPA, CFP®

INTRODUCTION

A MERICANS HAVE A UNIFYING CULTURE. It's what our unique and exceptionally prosperous country was built on: entrepreneurship.

"The archetypical Founding Father, pilgrim, creationist stories about the United States are all celebrating entrepreneurship," says University of Virginia business professor and entrepreneur Brendan Richardson.[1] "Pilgrims came to live here, struck out on their own into a completely unknown wilderness to create a new life. That's the entrepreneurial story right there."

On July 4, 1776, our Founding Fathers signed the Declaration of Independence, and if the war had gone a different way, this would have been our death warrant. Instead, it was a proclamation to leave oppression and create a new nation, and to this day, that spirit of independence is celebrated across the country. "If you've inherited your money here, good for you, but you didn't really deserve it," says Richardson. "You only really get credit for it if you've taken that inherited wealth and created more of it."

The American Dream holds that in return for hard work and perseverance, anyone can be successful, and Richardson has taken it to heart: "Starting in elementary school, we're all told that in this country, any one of us can grow up to be president someday. That has a hugely powerful effect that we don't really fully appreciate until you go to another country where that's crazy talk." During Richardson's many years overseas, he found that the idea of entrepreneurship is not as well received in Europe. "Being an entrepreneur means that you are a black sheep. You're swimming against the stream, you're not a good soldier, you're not a good member of society, you're an outcast. If you become successful, then all is forgiven. But failure is not tolerated there the way it is here. In the U.S., we love nothing more than a rags to riches story."

Today, Richardson lives in Charlottesville, Virginia, a place steeped in history, where Thomas Jefferson built Monticello and founded a university that operated outside the influence of the church.[2] Richardson says there's a bit of European traditionalism in the attitude of those who call the town home: "Charlottesville is beholden to its history, and in love [with] and mesmerized by its history, which is a problem. It's an inhibitor to thinking about what's new, what's next, what's the next big thing." In terms of disposition, Northern California's Silicon Valley forms a perfect foil, filled with talented, motivated individuals on the lookout for the "next big thing." Richardson knows from his two decades as a Bay Area resident that an idea written on the back of a napkin can turn into a multibillion-dollar company in a matter of years.

This classically American entrepreneurial spirit is still alive and well at Buck's, the famous Woodside, California, restaurant. Just as models, celebrities, and well-connected businesspeople glided through the velvet rope to disco dance at Studio 54 in the late 1970s, venture capitalists (VCs) and entrepreneurs have pitched multimillion-dollar deals over breakfast at this Silicon Valley hotspot since the 1990s.

After some lean times during the dot-com bust, Buck's still does a bustling business. During one of my interviews for this book, conducted over breakfast, my source told me to look around the room and said, "There are at least three or four ideas being pitched to VCs right now." For this book, I wanted to understand: What is the secret of personal financial success in Silicon Valley? As I know from my experience running a nightclub after college, when you own the place, you get to know your clientele—so it seemed only natural that Buck's proprietor, Jamis MacNiven, caught my attention and my ear.

Jamis MacNiven: More than a Pancake Guy

"Do you know where I can find socks for my pink alligator?" asked MacNiven after settling his tall, thin body into the booth where I was conducting an interview. My source and I played along: "Where is your alligator? How big is it? Does it need these socks to stay warm?"

Creative and insightful, MacNiven is a restaurateur, sculptor, storyteller, and former woodworker, just to name a few of his talents.[3] He welcomes people to his whimsical local haunt, which is chock-full of toy airplanes hanging from the ceiling, artwork covering the walls, and framed photos and tchotchkes accompanied by humorous captions. For example, the placard below a framed California license plate reading GOOGLE reports, "I was too dumb to buy the stock but I bought the plate."[4] Similarly, his playful business card humbly reads, "Just the pancake guy," underneath a picture of a King Kong–like ape climbing to the top of a giant stack of flapjacks, the creature's arm waving in the air at an old-fashioned propeller airplane. Even the menus at Buck's are full of MacNiven's stories, ensuring that even a lone diner will be fed and entertained.

MacNiven is in a position to wander the tables and look for ideas to invest in,[5] since he's worked in the crosshairs of venture capitalists and entrepreneurs for decades. Buck's opened in 1991. It's a "little Podunk restaurant in a strip center between the hardware store and the tennis shop," as MacNiven writes in his book, *Breakfast at Buck's: Tales from the Pancake Guy*.[6] About a year later, MacNiven was approached by tech leader Bob Metcalfe, the founder of 3Com and creator of Ethernet,[7] and the experience became the catalyst for his restaurant's iconic stature. Metcalfe, a grateful MacNiven explains, "took me aside at the grocery store. I had just gotten started, the food was terrible, the service wasn't very good, and the place was kind of a dump. Other than that, we were great. But I had no illusions that I was lighting the world on fire. [Metcalfe] said, 'You really need to pay attention and build this business, because I don't think you understand what a gem you have. It's in the rough, but it can be polished.' And I really listened to what he said. I really focused on the business more." MacNiven is still amazed at how Metcalfe's "mini-mentoring"—MacNiven's words for a practice he says happens all over Silicon Valley in various forms—gave him "a good wake-up call" and ultimately changed his life—and life in the Valley.

THE BOOM AT BUCK'S

As the Internet took the world by storm during the 1990s, Buck's popularity also really took off. TV and movie crews showed up regularly, along with a steady stream of customers. By the late 1990s, the restaurant had become *the* place where world-changing deals were made.

A seminal event in the restaurant's history, today known as "Buck's beaming," occurred on a July morning in 1999, when PayPal received its first major financing using its own money-encryption technology. Co-founder Max Levchin stayed up for 72 hours straight to make sure the technology worked, finishing at 9 a.m.—just one hour before the scheduled 10 a.m. beaming. A $4.5 million payment from the VCs was transmitted via two PalmPilots: representatives from Nokia Ventures and Deutsche Bank held one device, while PayPal co-founder Peter Thiel held the other.[8] His PalmPilot successfully received the venture funding using the very technology he and his co-founders created.[9] And it happened at Buck's.

What's the secret of this mecca? According to MacNiven, "It's just an accident of timing and geography and art. People like to come to a place that's energetic, where they're comfortable and they can stay as long as they like. We just happen to be next to Sand Hill Road, and the Internet happened to evolve around here. So, it's just a happy set of coincidences." He continues, "I've always felt like a cheerleader for Silicon Valley through its ups and downs, because I really am a believer. I think that all adds together. And people like to eat . . . We have food—I forgot about that."

DIVING EFFORTLESSLY INTO THE MINDS OF VENTURE CAPITALISTS & ENTREPRENEURS

Very few people have MacNiven's vantage point—watching the movers, shakers, and game changers in their rare off-hours, when they're just looking for some comfort food before venturing back out into the Valley. So he can offer some unique and rather unconventional insights regarding the difference between the first dot-com boom and today: "For a long time I thought that we'd learned a lot, and that we'd be smarter, and we wouldn't be hysterical about things like Facebook stock. In the end," he sighs, "I don't think we've learned a heck of a lot. I don't think we're able to learn much . . . I think the billionaires are younger and richer than ever, I think the valuations are crazier than ever, the speculation is every bit as risky as it's always been, and that it will rise, and it will pop, and it will fall again."

BILLIONAIRES AT BUCK'S

Today, MacNiven is acquainted with plenty of wealthy people and can attest to their unique apprehensions: "I do know more than one billionaire who's embarrassed by his money, who doesn't spend nearly what he could, and doesn't feel comfortable in the trappings," says MacNiven. "How do you treat your friends when you go to dinner? Do you then always start picking up the check, or do you not pick up the check, specifically, because you're the billionaire? I've been to dinner with more than one billionaire where I've picked up the check because they're trying to stay as normal as possible, and I congratulate them for that. Although," he cracks, "I'm perfectly willing to be purchased.

"For a long time, I thought it wasn't about the money," continues MacNiven, "and I still think that largely it isn't. But that presupposes that you get a whole big pile of money, and then you can make it not about the money. But until that point, it's kind of about the money. That's a large motivator." Yet, he sees plenty of people in the Valley pursue their goals with integrity and honesty. "What I think is important to a lot of people in the Valley is reputation above all else."

THE HEROES OF SILICON VALLEY

Like many of the interviewees for this book, MacNiven acknowledges the challenges of predicting a winner among the many budding startups. "Stuff is always popping up," he says, "almost like little particles in the froth of the universe, you know. They just keep popping up and exploding and disappearing."

Speaking about the role of venture capitalists in spotting the winners, MacNiven explains his admiration for their personal and professional risks: "A lot of the returns have not been that good for the investors; a lot of VCs have gone down. A third of them in the last 10 years that were around here are out of business. So they're risk takers. They're bringing us this bright future that seems to be what a lot of people want. I think they're to be celebrated just like the inventors, just like the entrepreneurs. They have a lot of [ideas] thrown at them, and they have to sort out what works, put some money in, and try to make it successful. The VC world has a specific structure, but the whole idea of listening to someone's idea, and financing them is as old as mankind. And there are lots of great examples, from Ferdinand and Isabella that sponsored Columbus—for good or bad, that was a VC-funded operation. That's been true of so many great enterprises. I think this industry is peopled with heroes."

As a friend to many VCs over the past two decades, MacNiven has observed some novel attempts to get funded. "I've seen so many funny things over the years. People actually cruising around with photos of VCs and trying to slap business plans on them like they were subpoenas, or something. If you're trying to get their attention as an entrepreneur, just have a good idea." VCs, he admits, "are only as good as the ideas people bring them. They're not trying to keep the ideas out. They're trying to keep out the people that will use their time unwisely.

"People come to Buck's, and they sit down, and they talk about the fabled elevator pitch—that does exist, and you should be able to tell your story to someone else, and they should be able to turn around and tell it to the person next to them, in three or four short sentences. If it doesn't lend itself to that in most of these areas, it won't get funded. One thing I've learned is that simplicity is truly king. From the hundreds of pitches I've heard over the years, I think that's the best lesson that I've extracted."

AN APOLOGY TO STEVE JOBS

Long ago—way before Buck's and just before Apple went public—Steve Jobs hired MacNiven as his general contractor,[10] and in the course of remodeling Jobs's home, MacNiven befriended the young computer genius. He remembers going couch shopping and car shopping with Jobs as frustrating and fruitless endeavors: "For years, he couldn't pick a couch because he'd rather sit on the floor than sit on a couch he didn't like." Nor did Jobs wish to compromise in his choice of car. And because there was no vehicle on the market with his ideal design and features, "Steve continued to drive his old Mercedes after his company went IPO." Eventually their friendship faded, as easygoing MacNiven found Jobs's indecisiveness in the name of perfection trying.[11] After Jobs's death, MacNiven acknowledged him in one of the Buck's menu stories: "Now that I am older, I really appreciate his persnicketiness. Steve wasn't in a position to teach me my trade, but he was a teacher. . . . So Steve, I'm sorry I wasn't a better craftsman. Now I get it, but alas it's too late."[12]

ENJOYING LIFE

MacNiven has concluded that working or doing good works gives life meaning and grants personal happiness: "Work is great. Without work, what do you do when you get up in the morning?" MacNiven asks. "A lot of people without work are pretty lost." Thus, MacNiven believes it's important for people to answer the questions "What's the purpose of life?" and "How do I measure success?" because, he explains "having your own jet doesn't make life 10 times nicer. Having the second jet doesn't make it better. We all know people with the jet, and they're not happier. . . . The interesting thing that I've learned all these years is that life is very simple. We try to extract all sorts of complexities from our environment, but really it's quite simple."

In a universe where everyone knows someone with a private jet, MacNiven's passions remain his artistic endeavors and creating new restaurants with his adult sons. After a breakthrough about his own longevity, he encourages people under 50 to take full advantage of the fact that life is "really long." Don't blow it all on rent or a house; instead, carve out a portion of your earnings from your salary or big liquidity event and use it to plan for your future, perhaps with a team of personal financial advisors. Following this strategy will be less stressful on you and your children in the future. "It may not feel like a lot now, but it will grow over time," says MacNiven.

"Are you living the life you want?" asks MacNiven. "If not, what are you waiting for?" He believes a lot of people will not honestly address these questions; however, he knows living a life that fulfills your passion is the key to happiness.

Sage advice from the pancake guy.

The Entrepreneur's Wheel of Life

Over a two-year period, I conducted more than 65 interviews with leading entrepreneurs, high-tech executives, and notables in order to find out what it takes for personal financial success in all stages of launching, building, and exiting a startup. Some sources are humble people who shun the spotlight but spoke as a favor to me or to a mutual friend. Many were happy to go on the record. Others were eager to protect their privacy and only felt comfortable discussing sensitive topics if I did not identify them by name. All have deep insights to share with you.

This book is organized around the Entrepreneur's Wheel of Life (see chart): The early days of a startup in Phase 1, ramping up to a liquidity event in Phase 2, a brief chapter on liquidity events, and the post-event period in Phase 3. After Phase 3, entrepreneurs typically return to Phase 1, where they are most fulfilled.

While many employees and executives who land a windfall stop working, most entrepreneurs never retire.

It's easy to assume wealth planning starts only after a liquidity event. However, as I explain throughout this book, windows exist early on in the life of a company that allow you to make decisions that could affect your net worth in a big way. After the event, new and surprising challenges appear. Having insight about what lies ahead is crucial for making good decisions. Whether you're a recent graduate starting your first company or a seasoned entrepreneur, understanding and planning around the Entrepreneur's Wheel of Life can help you make smart financial decisions about your personal wealth.

For executives and early employees who often move on to a Phase 4 once they've accumulated enough wealth (which might be through one large or several modest events), unique challenges and opportunities are explored in my book *Life, Liquidity & the Pursuit of Happiness: How to Maximize and Preserve Your Startup Wealth and Live Your Dreams.*

Here is a brief introduction to each phase.

PHASE 1: LAYING THE FOUNDATION

You'll enter Phase 1 with an idea that can change the world—or at least do something better or more brilliantly than anyone else. The months or years you spend building and growing your company are very exciting. It's during this time that you get your team together and test the viability of your product or service. You're also raising capital and taking in little or no income. Many people are preoccupied night and day with their startup to the detriment of their social life and health. This phase can also be very lonely and filled with doubt.

PHASE 2: RAMPING UP

For the lucky entrepreneurs who close in on a big wealth-creation event—an IPO, a sale, or a merger—you'll help negotiate the terms of the deal. Decisions made earlier about stock vesting and founders' agreements come into play here. You're still responsible for increasing the enterprise's value while you address the legal and financial implications of your deal. It's important to realize early on the ramifications of what you do with your personal equity awards.

The Entrepreneur's Wheel of Life℠

Pre-Transition Phase
2–40 years

1 Laying the Foundation

Challenges

QUALITY OF LIFE
- Preoccupation with startup
- Optimism
- Loneliness
- Improvisation
- Tenacity

FINANCIAL
- Raising capital
- Below-market salary
- Accountability to investors
- Funneling all resources into the company

Most entrepreneurs never retire.

They just keep going back to Phase 1.

Post-Transition Phase
1–24 months

3 Realizing the Dream

Challenges

QUALITY OF LIFE
- Figuring out what's next
- Determining how to return to Phase 1

FINANCIAL
- Accountability to shareholders, board, and management
- Increasing enterprise value
- Strategizing goals with financial resources
- Expensive purchases (home, car, jewelry, boat)

Pre-Transition Phase
0–24 months

2 Ramping Up

Challenges

QUALITY OF LIFE
- Maintaining balance while working long hours
- Excitement
- Persistence

FINANCIAL
- Negotiations
- Increasing enterprise value
- Compensation
- Learning new business skills
- Financial and tax planning
- Accountability to investors and board

LIQUIDITY EVENT

COMMON TO ALL PHASES

Challenge	Concerns	Solutions
Maximize Value of Equity Awards (ISO, NQ, RSA, RSU, ESPP)	Wealth Preservation	Financial Education
	Tax Reduction	Expert Team of Advisors
	Wealth Protection	Personal CFO
	Passing Assets to Heirs	
	Charitable Giving	

LIQUIDITY EVENT: THE PAYOFF

This is the time you've been waiting for. You and your team have received tangible financial proof that your company is valuable. Depending on which type of liquidity event you go through, what you experience in Phase 3 can vary.

PHASE 3: REALIZING THE DREAM

The two years following your company's liquidity event can bring on many changes. If you stay, things just won't be the same. Your work family may scatter, and you'll probably be subject to more oversight and accountability. The day-to-day routine may stay the same, but that startup, we're-all-in-this-together feeling usually fades. After the euphoria of sudden wealth brought on by your liquidity event has faded, entrepreneurs crave the chance to get back to Phase 1. You get to decide your next venture—and how to make sure you can afford it. You'll also have many opportunities to spend your wealth, including angel investing, expensive personal purchases, and your next startup.

PHASE 1
LAYING THE FOUNDATION

Pre-Transition Phase
2–40 Years

The Entrepreneur's Wheel of Life^{SM}

Pre-Transition Phase
2–40 years

1 Laying the Foundation

Challenges

QUALITY OF LIFE
- Preoccupation with startup
- Optimism
- Loneliness
- Improvisation
- Tenacity

FINANCIAL
- Raising capital
- Below-market salary
- Accountability to investors
- Funneling all resources into the company

Most entrepreneurs never retire.

They just keep going back to Phase 1.

Post-Transition Phase
1–24 months

3 Realizing the Dream

Challenges

QUALITY OF LIFE
- Figuring out what's next
- Determining how to return to Phase 1

FINANCIAL
- Accountability to shareholders, board, and management
- Increasing enterprise value
- Strategizing goals with financial resources
- Expensive purchases (home, car, jewelry, boat)

Pre-Transition Phase
0–24 months

2 Ramping Up

Challenges

QUALITY OF LIFE
- Maintaining balance while working long hours
- Excitement
- Persistence

FINANCIAL
- Negotiations
- Increasing enterprise value
- Compensation
- Learning new business skills
- Financial and tax planning
- Accountability to investors and board

LIQUIDITY EVENT

COMMON TO ALL PHASES

Challenge	Concerns	Solutions
Maximize Value of Equity Awards (ISO, NQ, RSA, RSU, ESPP)	Wealth Preservation Tax Reduction Wealth Protection Passing Assets to Heirs Charitable Giving	Financial Education Expert Team of Advisors Personal CFO

LAYING THE FOUNDATION

YOU MAY HAVE A COLLEGE DEGREE—or not—but you have a solution to a big problem and have started a company.

In Phase 1, persistence is key. If you're optimistic about your great idea for a product or service, you're ready to enter the Entrepreneur's Wheel of Life at Phase 1. Tips at the end of this section will help you to set your personal finances up for success as you build your company, understand the financial traps of startup life, consider the various methods of compensation for you and your team, and explore founder team dynamics that can impact your finances.

PROFILE
JONATHAN CARDELLA'S TRIP AROUND THE ENTREPRENEUR'S WHEEL OF LIFE

SOLD SKI WEST, INC. IN 2005[1] FOR $25 MILLION CASH PLUS EARNOUT.[2]

Jonathan Cardella's story is a classic example of the Entrepreneur's Wheel of Life: Identify a problem then solve it, build a company then monetize it, then repeat.[3] After his liquidity event at age 28, Cardella was lucky enough not to have to work again, but the event also created big problems he never could have anticipated before he started his company.

Cardella's Phase 1: Laying the Foundation

Jonathan Cardella has the street-smart business wisdom of someone decades older.

Upon graduating from Vanderbilt University in Nashville, Tennessee, Cardella was hungry to start his first business—only he wasn't sure what he wanted to do. He chose Park City, Utah, as home base, partially because of the forthcoming 2002 Winter Olympics in nearby Salt Lake City. "With the tourism and real estate industries being very strong there," he reasoned, "I knew that there must be a lot of opportunity for a business services provider."

Like most entrepreneurs, Cardella staffed up his first company with family and friends he convinced to move with him. His first company designed websites for the real estate and tourism industries. Although it boasted clients including Fortune 500 companies and one of the big ski resorts in town, he couldn't scale it.[4] He sadly realized his company was viewed as a commodity, like a lawn-mowing service: "You sweat, you bill an hour, you make a buck." Time to pivot and change.

Cardella spun off an online travel site that aggregated vendors in Park City into a one-stop search for vacation rentals. Ski West was launched on September 10, 2001. Considering the country's anguish after September 11, sales for the first three months of operations weren't bad. By the end of that year, the world had not ended, and the media was pitching an optimistic message about booking vacations on the Internet. Magically, Cardella remembers, "It was like somebody flipped the switch. [We] went from fifty thousand in revenue in three months to seven figures in the month of December."

Cardella quickly converted the rest of his team of salespeople, designers, and developers to Ski West employees. In the first quarter of 2002, they expanded to include other major ski markets, including Aspen, Vail, Jackson Hole, and Sun Valley. Within the first full year, revenue was approaching $10 million, and now the challenge was growth. To keep up with rising demand, the company had to quickly hire salespeople and programmers: "I kept recruiting my friends from

Vanderbilt," remembers Cardella, who is fortunately a very likable guy.

His charm—and the promise of future success—helped him amass his team, despite the below-market salaries he offered. Rapid growth continued for the next four years. Cardella remembers, "There were a lot of weekends when we were putting in call centers and building desks and setting up computers. I was scrambling to recruit and hire. But it was exciting and we knew we were building something great. We didn't know what the trajectory was exactly or where we'd end up."

Cardella describes this time as "a raging fire" that the team continued to feed. Ski West grew from 15 people to more than 100 employees, and saw triple-digit year-over-year growth. "There was a lot we didn't know," Cardella recalls, "but we just sort of figured it out as we went along."

Cardella's Phase 2: Ramping Up

The growth monster was eating cash like crazy. Cardella, along with a handful of his team, was personally financing the company, and everyone's cash reserves were very low. The team had stock, but no one knew what it was worth. That was when Cardella brought in the bankers.

Cardella was referred through a friend to a boutique investment bank in Silicon Valley, and rather than vet the firm, he trusted his friend and gave the bank a go. That bank provided guidance for marketing materials and financial models, introduced potential partners and acquirers, created a target list, and set up meetings for Cardella to pitch his company. This "road show" was a chance for Cardella to present to competitors in the online travel agency space and to private equity firms in an attempt to bring in financing for his cash-starved company. But he didn't like the terms of the offers coming in.

Giving the Bankers Indigestion

While Cardella was willing to wait to get the best offer, he got the sense the bank just wanted to close the deal. An extra $5 million would be really important to Ski West's shareholders, but for the bankers, $5 million may bring in only a few hundred thousand dollars in fees. Cardella acknowledges it "seems like a lot of money, but if you can do 10% of the work and always make a commission check, versus do incrementally five times more work and not know if you're going to get paid, it's obvious that feeding your deals off to private equity shops instead of dealing with strategics[5] and all the variables that go into a strategic purchase, makes a lot more sense to the banker." So Cardella took charge of the situation and suggested the bankers set up a meeting for him with a local Utah company, Overstock.com. He got the meeting, and it went right to negotiations. Cardella kept his cool and refused the initial offer, saying, "We don't take 5 p.m. deadlines on decisions this large. We don't think it's appropriate. We're fine if you don't want to do a deal with us. But we appreciate your interest." Eventually, after a one-on-one meeting with the Overstock CEO, Cardella got Overstock to double its initial offer.

The CEO-to-CEO pitch was the ticket to Cardella's deal. In the end, the self-confident Cardella was the best person to deliver his message.

Cardella's Phase 3: Realizing the Dream

All of the phases were challenging for Cardella, but Phase 3 was the toughest. "It was very disappointing," Cardella says about the surprising feelings he experienced. "Your whole life, this is what you want to do, and then one day you finally achieve it and you don't know what to do. You feel sort of despondent because everything you've been looking forward to, everything you've worked for, you've realized. And you kind of get lost."

Besides the lack of excitement, post-acquisition Cardella was "no more the top of the totem pole." Likewise, he was losing control of his baby, and subject to corporate bureaucracy and politics. This situation is anathema to so many entrepreneurs.

Culture Clash in Phase 3

Cardella was told that working at Overstock would be a lot of fun, and exciting times were ahead because there would be an emphasis on developing products to plug into the bigger platform; however, that was not the case. "The corporate environment is not very friendly to an entrepreneur," Cardella explains, "because an entrepreneur wants to come in and shake things up; they want to be successful at any cost. They're worried about the organization and the good of the organization." He contrasts this with the big corporate environment where "you have a lot of people in middle and upper management that want to maintain the status quo. And [who] aren't necessarily motivated by success because they don't see that success trickle right down to them. They have minimal [stock] options and they have a salary. They don't get paid for the success of the business always." When a startup is acquired by a large corporation, a damper gets put on the raging fire, and the wild growth stops.

"As an entrepreneur, you're seen as a threat. A liability," Cardella now understands. His goal is "to win and to make money for the business, and everybody else is more worried about when HR is crawling over everything you do to try to find how you somehow didn't dot some i or cross some t." The point is, public companies have more stakeholders and more regulations.

He expected his company, now a wholly owned subsidiary, to stay independent. Instead, it lost its identity and competitive edge, since Overstock was a big firm that already had a travel department. To Cardella, it was as if his company had died. He remembers, "We went from over 100% year-over-year growth to negative growth and decay," after the acquisition.

He stayed at Overstock just over two years. The first year was to satisfy his contractual obligation, and his second year was because he felt morally obligated to his friends who would lose their jobs if the company went bust. Plus, he did not want to tarnish his reputation by leaving behind a company with negative growth.

During this time, Cardella was given a mandate to restructure the business, and then to sell it. He hired the same investment bank, and went on another road show, this time for six months. His family life was disrupted and his partner left the state with their four-year-old child. Cardella became lonely and depressed, working in a company that had lost its soul without his family for support.

Finally, the optimist in Cardella resurfaced and he again tapped his personal connections to find a buyer. This time, Cardella's former company was sold to a private equity firm. But the terms of the deal were harsh on Cardella, including a multiyear, uncompensated non-compete agreement. Overstock.com still had $2 million in escrow from the original acquisition, so Cardella didn't want to derail the new deal. As he explains it, "I was non-competed out for two-and-a-half years, and I never got a dollar." Cardella hired an expensive lawyer, but because of Utah's pro-business climate, he suffered financially.

Personal Finances

Cardella advises entrepreneurs, "If you're going to give up control—or anywhere near control—you'd better get paid [in cash], because once you lose control, there's no telling what's going to happen." He favors cash over stock or earnouts, which are based on variables such as future profits.

As the filings and press releases about the sale of Cardella's company were made public, financial advisors came out of the woodwork, pressuring him to invest his proceeds. In retrospect, he wishes he had slowed way down and spent more time identifying and strategizing his personal life goals. Then, he could have determined how he could have deployed his financial capital to achieve his dreams.

He soon moved to San Francisco and got married. With help from his wise wife, who is a CERTIFIED FINANCIAL PLANNER™ professional, he carved out a fund in which capital would be preserved.

Despite the fact that he was now independently wealthy, he realized that for his happiness and sanity, his life needed a purpose. He needed to find his footing. Cardella knew he had gifts, and like most entrepreneurs, he wanted to take a risk and create another company—this time to solve a bigger, tougher problem. He ended up allocating a substantial amount of the cash portion of his sales proceeds to a segregated fund for his new venture, explaining, "I felt that I had an obligation to take a significant amount of the proceeds and invest them in myself, to put that money to work. If I just sat on it, I would be doing the wrong thing."

Phase 1, Again

Cardella is once again doing what entrepreneurs love most: he's building a new company. Fittingly, NeighborCity® satisfies a need Cardella discovered during his first trip around the Entrepreneur's Wheel of Life, when he identified the disconnect between investment bankers who are compensated to close a deal and their clients who are motivated to get the highest sales price. He realized that residential real estate sales have a similar model. Cardella's epiphany for moms and pops across the country is, "The real estate agent model is broken," because "the compensation structure [is] perverse with respect to the client's interest." His new company strives "to make the real estate market more liquid and transparent by creating a more effective means for people to identify the right person to get their home sold." He provides an example of this problem, and his idea about how to fix it:

> A $500,000 home is for sale and the owner wants to maximize his profit. To hold out for an additional $30,000 would translate to an extra $900 to the real estate brokerage, and perhaps $500–$700 of that goes to the real estate agent, on average.[6] This extra $700 is offset by the extra time on the market it will likely take to sell at the higher price, which brings with it increased costs for the agent. And there becomes a real risk that the deal won't happen if priced right at market rate. "That's a negative value that's a lot greater than the extra $700 that [the agent] might make by getting you the highest offer," Cardella calculates. To

fix the problem, NeighborCity® ranks real estate agents on their performance, based upon their clients' perspective, including getting the highest-possible sales price as quickly as possible. (For buyers, performance is based on getting the lowest purchase price and the execution of a smooth transaction.) The paradigm for rating a real estate agent is now defined by quality of outcome, not volume.

I'm hoping that Cardella will someday create a matching service to provide consumers with the tools to identify and evaluate financial advisors based upon their specific needs. Until then, he is enjoying his second time around the Entrepreneur's Wheel of Life.

The Golden Ticket: Great Team, Great Idea & Solid Financial Plan

Once committed to building a successful company, you need both an eager team and an idea worth getting excited about.

A handful of people I interviewed spoke about the challenge of finding good, yet affordable, talent for their startups. Savvy, young entrepreneurs gather their college friends to help with their first venture. Mid-career entrepreneurs keep in touch with former co-workers and team up later.

Regardless of enthusiasm, however, well-respected Silicon Valley transactional attorney Mark Cameron White contends that strength of concept is crucial to success: "In the Valley, ideas are still really important."[7] However, "you never get it right the first time around. So you need enough cash and time to get it right." White offers three pearls of wisdom for those building a startup:

❶ **Don't waste time building the wrong thing.** "There are seminars and books about how to develop for the market and get it out there quickly. You've got to know if your customer set is going to buy your solution, and you've got to know that right away. You don't want to waste your time. If you're wasting your time, you've got to redirect the ship and go in the right direction."

❷ **Financial planners and accountants can be of great help.** "There are lots of founding teams that break apart after a year when things get sticky," White says. To have staying power requires financial resources for the company, as well as a well-thought-out financial plan for both the amount of cash a founder can personally commit to the startup and his/her personal burn rate.

❸ **Determine how long the venture can be sustained before the cash runs out.** Funding is the perpetual problem of pre-public companies, says White. "Everybody always gets stuck on funding. It doesn't matter what stage of growth you're at, you're always looking at cash flow, how you're going to pay your people, how you're going to build a new initiative, what it's going to cost, what you can afford to do, and what are the proof points of what it is you're pursuing at that moment." And to get funding, White advises, "Investors like predictability. They like financial models that are based on some small data point that you can extrapolate from."

TWO RED FLAGS FOR FAILURE

A senior engineer with nearly three decades in Silicon Valley remembers the absolute, yet misguided, certainty about potential success felt by everyone on one of his early teams. After that experience, he suggests looking out for two main red flags for failure: Are you getting the product built? Is the team focused on getting the job done?[8]

What Makes Entrepreneurs Successful?

In 2009, the Kauffman Foundation, the world's largest foundation devoted to entrepreneurship, sponsored research precisely aimed at answering this question.[9] The report, entitled "The Anatomy of an Entrepreneur: Making of a Successful Entrepreneur," included a sample of 549 entrepreneurs from a range of industries—aerospace, defense, computer, electronics, health care, and service—who had made it past the startup stage. The researchers found that successful entrepreneurs were more likely to be males (92% of the sample) from middle-class backgrounds who had attained a greater amount of education than their parents. Of those entrepreneurs interviewed, 18% were born outside of the country, with the majority of those from India (4%) and the United Kingdom (2%). Most started their first company while married with children, predominantly citing financial and emotional reasons as their motivation.

Why did these entrepreneurs succeed? They attributed four factors integral to their accomplishments: luck, prior work experience, learning from past successes and failures, and management teams. The overwhelming reliance on luck is somewhat disheartening: 73% of the sample ranked good fortune as an important factor, 22% of whom said it was extremely important. The role of luck means that risking everything—like the majority of the sample who used personal savings to jump-start their own companies—should be done with eyes wide open.

Other components cited include faith in God, hard work, perseverance/determination, timing, spousal patience and support, optimism, and even a degree of naivety.

Importance of Company's Management Team

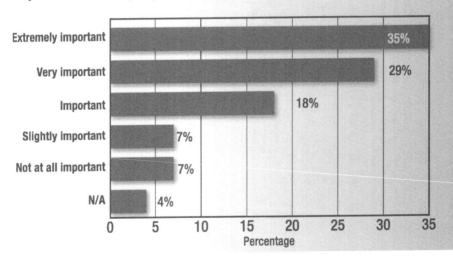

Figure 1: Founders value a strong team: 82% of respondents in a report published by the Kauffman Foundation indicated that a good management team is an important factor in their success, and 64% viewed it as either very important or extremely important.[10]

Ideal Timing: When to Start Your Startup

Many aspects of startup life come easier to the young, as one employee of dozens of burgeoning companies contends: "There's a life cycle to life in a startup. . . . You want to be young enough to have enough energy and enough naivety to respect the VCs."[11]

"If you're young, don't be afraid to do it," agrees Mark Galant, a 30-year veteran of startups and large multinational companies and a serial entrepreneur who built a company worth hundreds of millions.[12] By starting young, what you're giving up is an income. But you're gaining valuable hands-on experience. Twenty to 40 years ago, success seemed the only option, but "at this point in our society, there's almost no stigma for trying to start a company and failing," says Galant. He prefers to hire entrepreneurs, even if they've experienced failure. The "pre-kids" stage of life, says Galant, "is a good time to take the risk."

"Setbacks are not failures," concurs Roy Bukstein, who was part of the management team that took high-tech giant Oracle public.[13] "They are learning experiences." He encourages people to stretch their expectations and not to expect immediate success. Now in his early 60s, Bukstein finds that people change jobs more frequently, and loyalty is less important than it was 15 or 20 years ago—especially in the fast-paced environment of Silicon Valley.

MUSK'S MONEY STRATEGY

PayPal co-founder Elon Musk started his first company Zip2 in 1995, at the young age of 24. He shared his wealth preservation strategy with Knowledge@Wharton: "I had very little money, so there really wasn't any choice. I only had a few thousand dollars. We [Musk and his brother] just rented an office for $400 or $500 a month—some really tiny little office in Palo Alto. [It] was cheaper than an apartment. And then [we] bought futons that converted into a couch, which was sort of like a meeting area during the day. We would sleep there at night and shower at the YMCA, which was just a few blocks away. That was [an] extremely low burn rate. [It was] way cheaper than a garage. Garages are . . . expensive. So we were able to . . . putter along for several months until we got venture funding. I think that's a good lesson. When you are first starting out, you really need to make your burn rate ridiculously tiny. Don't spend more than you are sure you have."[14]

Fast-Paced Enterprise

While you're building your company, it's smart to keep an eye on your business rivals as well. These days, geographic barriers have come down and products can quickly be created and put on the market; likewise, "anybody can be a competitor" now, says Leland Fong, who recently retired after a 40-year career mostly spent at large financial companies working on payment solutions and at high-tech Silicon Valley companies like Intel.[15] "It used to be you had IBM competing against UNIVAC. There are no deterrents for players [today]." The challenge, says Fong, is that "the entry point is so low, now, to get into business," that products are developed overnight. Fong cautions that many people at companies with a hot product are blind to the potential competition that can sabotage sales at any moment—and he cautions that "companies can disappear overnight, too."

One reason why entrepreneurs work insane hours is to ensure they are the first to get their product to market. And if you've got a hot product, your situation could change overnight due to worldwide competition, fickle consumers, consolidation, or management changes. This mutability is all the more reason to understand your current personal financial situation, and to thoughtfully assess your path based on all known variables.

PROFILE
THE PHILOSOPHY OF PHIL LIBIN

LAUNCHED EVERNOTE IN 2008. RAISED MORE THAN $200 MILLION IN VENTURE CAPITAL, HAS 66 MILLION USERS, VALUED AT $1 BILLION.[16]

Prescient Evernote CEO and co-founder Phil Libin created and sold two companies before starting Evernote, a company with a 100-year business plan. Passionate about creating technology, shaping his company, and helping other entrepreneurs, Libin has a warm and bold presence and spoke without notes or slides when he delivered a keynote in front of hundreds of people at Vator Splash San Francisco, a startup pitch competition designed to accelerate entrepreneurs along the learning curve.[17]

A first-generation American, Libin warns that when you build a startup, you must be psychologically prepared to fail—and to recognize the consequences of the failure for those who may be depending on you, like your family. In light of the Silicon Valley pressure to innovate, his pithy advice to would-be entrepreneurs includes the idea that "almost all successful companies were not the first in their space," explaining, for example, that the first MP3 players got left in the dust when Apple created the ubiquitous iPod and iPhone. He believes entrepreneurs should focus on creating a new product or improving upon an existent technology, rather than simply taking market share away from an existing company.

Product-related challenges aside, executive responsibilities can take a unique toll on personal well-being. "Being a CEO is a lonely job," Libin explains in his speech, "but it beats having a job." When he's with other CEOs, going out for drinks after a long day of meetings and at other group gatherings, this issue of isolation always surfaces. Libin, who likes to be connected with his office when he's not physically there, playfully uses a roving robot that wanders through the workplace to keep employees on their toes.[18] Still, he explains, those looking for power as a CEO of a startup will be disappointed, because your power is "an inverted pyramid; everyone is your boss, including VCs and the media."

Six Questions of Entrepreneurship

Before plunging in to start a company, Libin proposes entrepreneurs ask themselves—and answer—six crucial questions:

❶ **Who?**—Are you the right kind of person for entrepreneurial life? "Don't do it for the money, or the freedom," Libin advises, as statistics prove the low success rate of startups. Plus, he quips, "you get flexible time—you can work any 20 hours of a day you want!"

❷ **Why?**—"To change the world." Or, to quote Steve Jobs, "We're here to put a dent in the universe."[19]

❸ **When?**—"When the world has just changed and an important problem has gone from being impossible to just really, really hard," he says, "that's the best time to create a product."

❹ **Where?**—The best place to begin your startup is where "your best friends, who are willing to work long hours for free, are at." Libin lived in Boston for the first 19 years of his career before moving to the Bay Area.

❺ **What?**—"Find something that lots of people are doing that is not a great experience and make it a little better."

❻ **How?**—"Ignore conventional wisdom."

I heard Libin's keynote a year and a half into my research for this book; all of my interviews were done typing notes into Evernote on my iPad, syncing my notes in real time as I typed to my desktop computer at my office and on my iPhone. Brilliant technology, and brilliant wisdom.

Thank you, Phil Libin.

Founder Team Dynamics

Maybe you dropped out of college, moved to California, live in a tiny apartment with your co-founders, and work nonstop. You care about your company and are part of a team that believes in a shared goal: to grow the company and create value.

That kind of positive energy is a terrific asset as you move through Phases 1 and 2 toward a liquidity event. "One thing that you really need to be careful about—and it has happened with several of my [client] companies—is founder disputes," warns Stephanie Coutu, an attorney focused on venture capital financing, mergers and acquisitions (M&A), and intellectual property transactions at Arnold & Porter in San Francisco.[20] What happens when the partner who you thought you could work with forever turns out to get bored, or not live up to expectations? Coutu's advice: "Up front, you need to have very defined expectations and roles for founders," because not all individuals involved in the beginning are as equal, or as valuable, to a company.[21]

Therefore, setting expectations early on is key. Here are some questions startup attorney Michael Irvine suggests addressing when you're part of a founding team:

- Who's going to be in charge of key decisions?
- What are you trying to achieve?
- Are you trying to maximize the up-front vested portion for the founders?
- Are you trying to put in place a framework that's going to survive VC scrutiny? Because you're going to negotiate your vesting when you're taking on financing.
- How is the equity ownership going to be split between the founding team?
- When will you allow investors? (Or will you?)
- How shall you slice and dice the options vesting?
- Who will own the intellectual property? (Irvine recommends that the company own it.)
- What if one founder needs to leave or take time away from the business because of something unexpected, such as an illness?
- What acceleration types will be allowed?[22]

During these discussions, remember to look out for yourself and your career: "The title of founder means zero," contends Irvine. "It's pure reputation. You can put it on your résumé, but look up the Delaware code, or the California corporations code. There's no title of founder. It has no power. It's not in any corporation's bylaws. It's important to know, really, what your role and rights are. California is pretty employee-friendly, but at the end of the day, you can be terminated at will. No one has the right to continued employment. So that's going to affect your vesting and your ownership."

Coutu notes that "sometimes there's a conflict between what's best for the founder and what's best for the company," because the company wants to make itself as attractive as possible for a purchase, while the "best thing for the founder may be something different, depending on the purchase price or the founder's individual circumstances."

Drafting founders' agreements with an attorney should address the following issues early on:

- What will happen to the company and the stock if you or your co-founder(s) want to leave?

- In the event of a death or disability, what happens to that person's stock? (If there are no agreements in place and your co-founder dies, the stock transfers to his or her beneficiaries. In other words, without an agreement in place, you could end up in business with your co-founder's parents, spouse, or kids!)
- Put a Proprietary Information and Inventions Agreement (PIIA) in place that says founders, employees, and consultants agree that anything they develop while they're working for the company belongs to the company. VCs want to see this arrangement, and it maximizes the company's value. But if the founder leaves the company, "once you have assigned [the IP] to a company and the company gets financing or gets acquired, the IP is not yours to do anything with," cautions Coutu.
- What happens upon a change of control? If the company is bought, does the founders' vesting get accelerated? This is where single and double triggers come into play. (See page 29 for a discussion of triggers.)

Bringing In an Attorney

Phases 1 and 2 are vital times to protect your human and intellectual capital—so on day one of any business venture, hire a legal team. "Most legal firms have a startup package," says one very successful engineer and entrepreneur.[23] "It goes into setting up an option plan and offer letters. It goes into single trigger, double trigger. It goes into setting up employment contracts. It's a standard package that most Silicon Valley firms have that I've leveraged a couple different times. And I think that's the right way to do it."

WHY HIRE AN ATTORNEY?

While you're busy creating your company, addressing legal issues like founders' agreements and equity vesting early can save you a lot of headaches and financial trouble down the road.

"To fix what has been done incorrectly can take a long time and a lot of money. And some things you can't fix," warns Coutu. VCs will want to see that there are agreements in place with reasonable vesting schedules, and, she adds,

"If you have no vesting arrangement on your shares in place, then [the VCs] are likely to impose one, and it's going to be a lot harsher than the one that you put on yourself."

VCs also want to eliminate negotiation with an acquiring company about the stock or options vesting of founders and early employees. "They don't want you to have that leverage on the liquidity event," says Michael Irvine. "So they're fighting you in the pre-transition Phase 2. They can't fight you at the formation stage because they're not at the table yet. But when they come in and make their investment, they're reviewing your stock purchase agreement and your acceleration. They'll write it into the term sheet [for the investment or acquisition] as 'founder vesting shall be as follows.' Most VCs are very rigorous in this regard. It then gets negotiated."

SINGLE & DOUBLE TRIGGERS IN AN ACQUISITION

Having worked on mergers and acquisitions (M&A) at a large law firm early in her career, and as an in-house attorney working in the trenches on four liquidity events, Kate (name changed to protect her privacy)[24] has seen many high-tech deals go down, and offers her unique insight regarding the legal issues executives and early employees are likely to encounter when joining a startup.

Negotiating to go into a company, it's important to understand what happens to your equity awards if there's a company acquisition or merger. A "single trigger" means all your options accelerate upon the change in control event. In reality, though, you're more likely to have a double-trigger situation.[25] A double trigger is the acceleration of unvested shares based upon two events: an acquisition of the company and the employee's termination. When an acquisition or merger occurs, an employment agreement for a startup executive will generally address the following issues:

- Options vesting—a single trigger is preferred over a double trigger
- A gross-up cash payment to cover tax liability if you're hit with the excise tax, or a restructure of your equity awards, so that you don't get hit with the excise tax
- Severance payment, if you're terminated[26]

While it's more common to have a double-trigger event upon a change in control, "how the double trigger is structured is really important," says Kate. "Say, they keep you on because they don't want to pay you, but you no longer have any of the same duties—you're basically just there so they don't have to accelerate your options, but you have nothing to do—that's not uncommon. Or, they'll keep your title just so your options don't accelerate. You want to be sure that your employment contract is structured with a number of different triggers. Even if there's a constructive termination [a situation in which an employee resigns because the employer's behavior is intolerable],[27] or you have a major change in duties post-acquisition, you want to have the option to leave and your options accelerate."[28]

UNVESTED EQUITY TRIGGERS

The two triggers that can cause acceleration of unvested equity are as follows:

1. **Change of control.** For example, if the company is sold or merged. "You were CEO of your startup, but when Google buys you, you won't be CEO of Google. But if Google is buying your company, it's going to usually become a division. Then, you should still be head of that division or something close to it," says attorney Irvine.

2. **Leaving the company.** There are different permutations, including if you leave the company or if you were fired (with or without cause, and how cause is defined). "If the company didn't fire you," says Irvine, but you got demoted "from head of sales to head of janitorial services, that's kind of a different job. Not what you signed on for. You're effectively fired at that point."

Emerging growth company attorney Danny Krebs of Alliance Counsel says the opportunity to resign for "good reason" should be part of the second trigger.[29] For example, if you have a reduction in salary or a material change in duty, resigning with good reason will get you the second trigger and preserve your equity awards. Having an attorney read your employment contract is your best protection.[30]

As he pounds the Phase 1 section of my chart with vigor, Irvine says Phase 1 is the best time to get acceleration of stock options written into your employment contract. These days, "boards have more discretion and flexibility over what happens to unvested equity upon change of control," he says. "And now what we're seeing is boards actually have full carte blanche. Unless you have contractual acceleration [where] it's written into your agreement, when the company gets bought, anything that's unvested could completely disappear into the ether."

Irvine knows of "hundreds of thousands of stories of that happening" and advises executives to push for contractual acceleration. "The VCs are focused on building liquidity to return money to their LPs [limited partners], so they want to maximize all of the talent value in the enterprise, build the enterprise value, get it sold or take it public, and get out. That doesn't jive with the founder who's trying to build up the enterprise, and who may want to take it to the next level, take it public, and hold on to it." Irvine notes, "The VCs have 100% acceleration. When the company gets bought, they're getting 100% liquidity." He advises founders and executives to fight for their rights in Phase 1, at formation. Irvine urges his founder clients to ask for 100% double trigger.

PAYING YOUR ATTORNEY:
DEFERRAL OR A PIECE OF THE ACTION?

Be sure to consider which kind of law firm and payment schedule might be your best fit. Some large law firms that advise startups in Phase 1 are willing to defer a portion of the fees until funding occurs, according to my interview sources.

Smaller firms may act differently. Mark Cameron White of White Summers says his deep knowledge base keeps clients coming back to him. "Our law firm discounts services to get a small stake in selective companies. We don't do it across the board; we're very selective. A lot of firms did that and are out of business now." Instead, he takes a little bit in a wide variety of companies and then diversifies the equity he's gotten over the years into more conservative investments, such as publicly traded securities. White uses his intellectual capital to make investments in startups. "Time is money in my business, because I'm doing stuff for free that I could charge for." For this reason, White and his partners "cherry-pick our companies. We want to work with people that appreciate us and pay us. We want to work with companies that we think are going to change the world."

See my book *Life, Liquidity & the Pursuit of Happiness* for more details on how attorneys can help your startup prepare for and achieve success while mitigating unpleasant surprises.

Expanding Your Skill Set

Most founders are expert at one or two things, like engineering or finance, but in the intense startup environment you have to wear many hats and become knowledgeable in new areas. One engineer and entrepreneur who spoke to me off the record avers that in each new venture he's "constantly playing catch-up and learning."[31] For example, he had to learn how to run a sales force, and how to run a human resources department. "There's always a learning curve in Phase 1, depending on what you're biting off," he says.

Because resources are tight, you're spending time to understand areas beyond your education or training: "I was going home at night and reading HR documents," recalls the engineer and entrepreneur, "and reading up on how to grow sales forces. I was going home at night and learning about CRM tools, and stuff that in my life as a VP of Engineering I wouldn't have cared less about. I was fortunate enough to have been through funding a number of startups by the time I was a CEO—but I know other folks who are going home and are learning about liquidation preferences and cap tables and dilution and antidilution and legal terms and contract negotiations." The lesson for founders is to understand your strengths, and that your business challenges will likely be in areas that are not your strengths. He explains it this way: "Everyone I know who has been in Phase 1 who have been new entrepreneurs have always realized that there's a big, huge can of worms there that they haven't necessarily opened before."

From day one, in addition to their technical expertise, founders need business expertise. Even if the outside help is just a few hours a year, wisdom from other entrepreneurs and business advice from professional service providers, such as attorneys, CPAs, and contract CFOs, is crucial. Talking with an expert or someone more experienced is especially beneficial to a first-time entrepreneur.[32] Many of the successful entrepreneurs I interviewed enjoy helping others. So the mentor-mentee relationship is a win-win for everyone.

Challenges Faced by Founders in Starting Their Business(es)

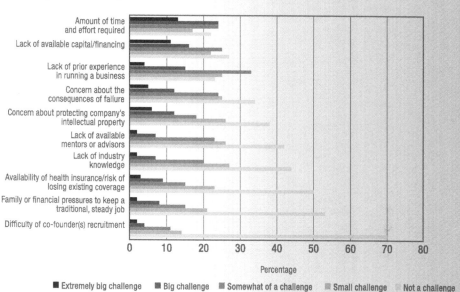

Figure 2. The largest challenges faced by founders in starting their business, as ranked by 549 entrepreneurs in the Kauffman Foundation report. (Wadhwa et al.; *The Anatomy of an Entrepreneur: Making of a Successful Entrepreneur.*)

What can get in the way of entrepreneurial success? In the Kauffman Foundation report cited earlier, researchers asked 549 founders to rank the various challenges they faced when starting their companies.[33] Overall, they were very optimistic. A majority deemed the following factors "somewhat of a challenge" or greater: time and effort, lack of capital, and lack of experience in running a business. However, few ranked even these problems as "extremely big challenges." The biggest obstacle turned out to be the amount of time and effort required, at 13%. (See Figure 2.)

Given the acknowledged difficulty of entrepreneurship, a surprising discovery was that most entrepreneurs considered fear of failure, protecting intellectual property, having few mentors, lack of industry knowledge, loss of health insurance, family pressures, and co-founder recruitment "not a challenge." In fact, some founders pointed to naivety as a success factor because it masks many of the true challenges.[34]

PROFILE

THE CURIOUS ENTREPRENEUR: PETER HERZ

SOLD 3WARE IN 2004 TO APPLIED MICRO CIRCUITS CORPORATION FOR $150 MILLION IN CASH.[35]

Peter Herz loves learning.

With a wide, friendly smile, he finds satisfaction by creating companies and helping other entrepreneurs, because it expands his own knowledge.[36] A Carnegie Mellon graduate in electrical engineering and mathematics,[37] Herz is a true entrepreneur and Renaissance man whose expertise includes engineering, investing, mentoring, board service, and writing. Entrepreneurship runs in his blood; his dad was an entrepreneur. Thus, startups—and risk taking with his own human capital—come naturally. He's also a clear and articulate speaker and a voracious reader.

In 1997, Herz and Jim McDonald[38] founded 3ware, a data storage company. In 2004, Applied Micro Circuits Corporation acquired 3ware for $150 million in cash. In between was a very long process to get the company off the ground and bring in the first round of venture capital. "I tend to work on very unsexy projects, because I like finding things that have real value propositions around them," says Herz. He mentions this as a counterpoint to many hot companies like Google and Facebook that are "built on advertising, so they do one thing to collect their users, and then they make their money on selling that to other people," and a disconnect exists. "I prefer to work on businesses that have a direct value proposition, where your customers and the people you're providing value to are really the same population," Herz explains.

On Entrepreneurship

In Herz's estimation, many entrepreneurs and VCs try to "figure out what's hot. And if you try to build a company around that as your foundation, then you're likely to be disappointed, because those things change pretty quickly in the time it takes to build a company." He points to Phase 1 on the chart and agrees that the time it takes to build a company is two to 40 years. "I think you have to want to build a company for noneconomic reasons," Herz explains. "If you are doing it for what you think is a big economic win, at the end of the day, you're very, very likely to be disappointed. It's an economically irrational act to start a company. If you want a good outcome economically, risk-adjusted, stay in a big company, take a nice big salary, and you're all set. Startups," he cautions, "are not an economically smart move."

Herz then mentions his college friends, who just out of school took jobs at large companies where they worked on a very tiny part of a large project. He contrasts this with his determination to be an entrepreneur. "I like being on a really steep learning curve."

Financing the Startup

At first, Herz's company consisted of just six people. Outside financing was slow to obtain, but about six months after incorporating, 3ware raised a very small amount—a few hundred thousand dollars. At that point, 3ware paid each employee $2,000 a month. Raising money from venture capitalists was really hard to do in the late 1990s. Herz explains: "In the aftermath of the Netscape IPO, everybody was looking at eyeballs and clicks, and the information superhighway—that was what was hot, even though all of that had to start and end somewhere, and therefore there was the implication that the data storage to support that would be enormous. [But] that wasn't where people were looking to fund at the time.

"We pitched one [VC] firm focused on the Internet. We walked in with a little prototype board of what we're building, because it is part hardware, and the partner called over to his other partner and said, 'Hey look, these guys are building something.' They had never actually seen a piece of hardware in their firm before." 3ware was eventually funded by New Enterprise Associates (NEA).

Startup Life

Herz loves working with too few people, because it means "you end up doing things you haven't done before. What gets me out of bed in the morning is learning. That's my motivation. The people who are rational about this type of pursuit understand that it's not about an economic outcome." But having too few people also means long hours, loneliness, and stress.

On Family

Two-career couples often face more time challenges than families with a stay-at-home spouse. Herz spent time at home with his two sons right after his liquidity event but soon started another company. "There are a couple of challenges, and the way my wife and I organize it is we describe how hard our work lives are in a particular gear, between the first and fourth gear—first is you're not working, and fourth is it's all-out. We decided early on that we would never both be in the fourth gear at the same time, so we try to switch off to have some overall balance."

Herz's sons are continuing the family tradition of reading, and no matter how hectic his schedule, he and his sons read together (his oldest is 14) every night.

A Sandwich as a Salary

After working for others for 12 years, Herz started and personally bankrolled his company with his co-founders. "The compensation plan at that point was if you came to work we bought lunch, and if you stayed late we bought dinner." There was also equity, but no salary. Their team was "very eclectic," composed of people the co-founders knew who were between projects. "We talked to a number of people who were intrigued with the idea of joining a startup." However, "it is a very sobering moment when you put a $0 offer letter on the desk." It was clarifying to remove salary from the equation. "I had a number of people who did not join at the time because, for some, it didn't make sense, and for other people, it wasn't the right time in their lives, [or] in their careers, to make that kind of step. If you've got a family, you can't do that." In the end, "We built a small team of committed, potentially insane people."

Working collaboratively with a fierce belief in the company's product, the team's optimism fueled its expectations for a financial payoff. The employees were betting their human capital on equity, rather than salary. And the gamble paid off well for early employees.

"I'm actually an optimistic guy, and that's why I do startups," says Herz proudly.

Compensation and Cash Management

As Peter Herz's story affirms, the payoff for founding a startup is not a lucrative salary but the equity compensation **after** a liquidity event, so it is important that entrepreneurs are able to survive—and avoid bankrupting their own futures—while they follow their passions. Whether you're sleeping in your office or being paid with a sandwich, make sure you realize your personal financial risk, translated as low or non-existent savings during the startup years, in case things don't go according to plan.

HOW ENTREPRENEURS MANAGE CASH

The seasoned startup veterans I spoke with warned against sinking too much of your own savings into your company because of the already inherent financial risk of working at a startup. However, many entrepreneurs discussed the need for flexibility with their cash flow for investment opportunities in startups, and a few suggested novel, seemingly counterintuitive ways to make sure that they stay flexible to raise cash easily.

"As an entrepreneur," says Tesla Motors founder Martin Eberhard, "I need to be able to at-will ratchet my mandatory expenses down to minimum."[39] While he admits there are always necessary expenses, such as "property taxes, food, and gas," he prefers to avoid a mortgage: "If I don't have a mortgage, then I don't have to pay a mortgage payment, and on top of that [the bank] can't force me to buy house insurance. So I can cut off my insurance, I can [choose] not to insure my cars, [or even sell them]." At his discretion he'll buy insurance on his cars and home, although forgoing car, home, or umbrella liability insurance is very risky, because your future wealth can be tapped to pay for an at-fault accident. "If things got bad in a startup situation" and the business needed the cash, Eberhard explains, "I could stop paying. I actually do carry homeowner's insurance, although I'm careful about it. I get very high deductibles, and I looked very carefully at earthquake insurance and decided it's a rip-off. If my house gets smashed, I'll fix it myself."

WHAT IT MEANS TO FOCUS ON THE MONEY

Planning is crucial, yet entrepreneurs should not focus solely on their potential payout, as Sylvia Yam, former Wall Street and Silicon Valley M&A dealmaker, explains: "That's not the kind of person that a company wants to hire. . . . If I were the acquirer, I would be like 'no thanks.' It's not worth it. I can pay a lot of money to anybody who will build something for me and will stick around. But it's always a red flag when you're an acquirer if you meet someone that is not strategically focused, that's only personally focused and has no incentive to stick around."[40] Yam has a unique perspective on mergers and acquisitions. She was an M&A analyst at JPMorgan in New York before moving to California to work on corporate development for Yahoo. In three years at the Sunnyvale-based Internet pioneer, she closed about 10 deals, "ranging from $1 million to $4 billion," she remembers.

VC Sonja Hoel Perkins expands on this: "If you're the type of person who is focused on your annual take-home pay, then being an entrepreneur is not for you."[41]

On the other hand, while avoiding talk about money allows for deeper interactions with friends and colleagues, neglecting personal finances can spell trouble. Too often, busy do-it-yourselfers can get into trouble running on financial autopilot. Although they may be able to successfully manage their own money, they might get blindsided or miss out on crucial opportunities. At the end of the day, success relies on building a great product with a great team, good fortune, and making smart financial decisions along the way to secure your future wealth.

EQUITY COMPENSATION AT STARTUPS

Today, many startups issue options, but more mature companies (that may not have even gone through an IPO) usually award restricted stock as compensation. With stock options, recipients must choose when to exercise and when to sell. However, with restricted stock, it's simple: you vest and own the shares when the restrictions lapse, and you owe tax at that time. A detailed description of equity award types begins on page 49.

SERIES FF STOCK

Here's a bitter irony of the high-tech world: Founders of successful companies are often cash poor. Their businesses may be growing at an exponential rate, but their bank balances are alarmingly low.

Investors and entrepreneurs should take note of this cautionary tale: Mark Galant, a serial entrepreneur profiled on page 96 talked about the frustration of having 95% of his net worth tied up in his very successful company. Because of this, he acted "way too cautiously and conservatively" and wished he had taken more risks with the company, including spending a lot more on marketing. Interestingly, he had already achieved a moderate amount of business success before starting his company, and he had a multimillion-dollar net worth outside of the business to show for it. His startup was yielding a profit margin of almost 50%, and his investors were up 70-fold for every dollar they had put in.

More surprisingly, when he looks back on this time, he remembers thinking "As long as I have all my net worth in this [company], I'm going to make bad decisions when it comes to the business." Galant also recalls, "At that point, I was the biggest shareholder, and I finally convinced [the board to raise money]." The company did a handful of financing rounds over a few years, and, he adds, "As it turns out, I think they were afraid I might take the money and go off to Argentina and never be seen again. But I worked just as hard after I raised money as I did before I raised the money. And the company still continued to do well under my purview."

In light of sticky situations like these, a relatively new share class has emerged to allow founders to sell some stock early on, before the liquidity event. Known as Series FF stock, it was invented by the Founders Fund, a venture capital firm started by three founders of PayPal. When the PayPal team was building its own company, the members wanted cash to pay their rent, but the company's VC firm believed "a hungry CEO is a more effective CEO. Let a founder take some cash out early, they argue, and you risk diminishing his commitment and drive."[42] Series FF stock is a type of preferred stock created as a way to satisfy both the needs of entrepreneurs who may have their entire net worth tied up in their company, and are therefore racking up hefty credit card bills with interest charges just to pay for their living expenses, and VCs who would like control of their own eventual cash-outs, while retaining the founders and early employees to build the company. A Series FF stockholder can essentially sell these shares to investors during a round of financing.[43]

Having an opportunity to do so, but not taking action to cash out at least a modest amount early on is where an entrepreneur's enthusiasm may become dangerous. As a proponent of avoiding a concentrated position in one stock or company, I believe early diversification is preferable. But there's a balance between giving up too much upside by selling too early, and the cautious path of diversification. Generally, Series FF shares allow founders to take a few chips off the table.[44] With this cash, you may even begin to set up a segregated pot of funds to preserve some of your capital for your most crucial needs and help secure your financial future (see page 110 for more on the "buckets"). Most founders will want to keep a hefty chunk of their net worth in the company pre-liquidity, but there's a big difference between 50% of your net worth and 95% of your net worth tied up in one venture. Besides, taking some money off the table is usually a prudent way to protect your net worth if your company crashes and burns.

In their white paper "To Buy or Not to Buy? Giving Founders Early Liquidity," Sarah Reed and Peter Fusco explain that "the impetus for a partial cash-out of a founder may also come from investors—for example, investors seeking to deploy more capital and get more ownership in a Web 2.0 deal, where the company's low cash burn makes it debatable whether VC funding is needed at all."[45] There are important legal, tax, and accounting issues involved in providing founders with early liquidity. And many investors are extremely averse to the concept. Therefore, "assume that the transaction will elicit strong reactions among at least some of your co-investors," write Reed and Fusco. Series FF stock is written into a company's charter from inception and is designed to solve some of the legal and accounting issues involved with owner cash-outs.

Getting cash out could take the form of a loan to the founders or a stock sale. Founders generally prefer a stock sale over a loan because of the following issues:

- Gain on a stock sale is taxed at favorable tax rates. However, the stock must be held for more than a year.
- Interest must be paid on a loan. If no interest is paid, then the imputed interest is considered income. (There are accounting issues to consider in this circumstance.)
- If a loan is later forgiven, the founder is taxed on the loan amount as ordinary income.
- Unless a loan is fully collateralized, usually via pledging the founder's common stock, the IRS may collapse the transaction and consider it a stock option for tax purposes. Section 409A may come into play to cause the transaction to be taxable upon receipt of the funds.[46] (Section 409A is a technical area beyond the scope of this book.)

Note: Series FF stock is used in Founders Fund deals. It is separate from Class F stock designed in 2009 by The Founder Institute to provide founders with special rights, such as super-voting rights upon incorporation.[47]

Funding Options for Your Startup

The good and bad news in the Internet age is that it costs $100,000 to start a company, says a VC source. Barriers to entry are low and outsourcing of coding tasks is fairly easy. If you're lucky, you can get a lot further without giving up as much of your company.[48] As a result of this interesting and relatively new phenomenon, alternative methods of raising capital have arisen in both Phases 1 and 2. If you have investors, you're always accountable to them; on the other hand, when the founders raise money, only insiders (and their friends) control company ownership, and dynamics of the collaboration come into play.

When do you need to raise capital? It's more common today than a decade ago for founders not to raise capital, and then get an earlier exit. Companies often get acquired earlier on in their lives because they haven't taken angel or venture capital money, in which case the exit may not be as big, but it can still be attractive.

Venture Capital

Although the process can appear "a little opaque to most engineers," according to one source,[49] venture capital greases the wheels of the Bay Area economy, so it is crucial to know how to make intelligent financial decisions on both the giving and receiving end of VC funding.

For the uninitiated, a venture capitalist is an investor: in return for cash, VCs take a piece of your company, and their ownership percentage determines their amount of power. VCs generally invest in multiple companies at a time. Each VC fund contains a pool of money from multiple investors, called a portfolio, and individual companies within it are known as portfolio companies. In contrast to VCs, private equity firms use money from pension funds and extremely high net-worth individuals to buy large stakes in companies and then actively run the companies they acquire.

The entrepreneurs I talked to often held strong opinions about VC funding. The majority preferred to take money from VC investors so that they could hire talent and quickly grow the company, while the minority believed VC funding was a necessary evil. And an even smaller percentage believed in bootstrapping—funding the venture solely from their own pockets, with some help from friends and family—and refusing to take VC money, in order retain control and to avoid answering to a board of directors picked by an outsider.

A VC'S PERSPECTIVE

Lara Druyan started her career on Wall Street but didn't like being a banker. Through research and informational interviews, she found that for people who like technology, enjoy building things, and are intellectually curious, venture capital is "a real privilege of a job, because entrepreneurs tell you their dreams." Now, Druyan controls her destiny by choosing who she works with, favoring big-idea entrepreneurs who share how "their company is going to change something, make something better, do something that didn't exist before."

A POPULAR PATH: ENTREPRENEUR TO VC

One wildly successful serial entrepreneur I spoke with says he's been thinking about delving into VC or private equity, "because they don't have to work those 90-hour weeks. . . . They can still take vacation, they can still mentor younger people, they can still give advice, and they can still make good money. But it's just not the all-encompassing thing that you have [when you are] running your own business."[50]

AN EXECUTIVE'S PERSPECTIVE

While many VCs relish the ability to foster companies, a retired high-tech sales executive with plenty of experience on the receiving end of VC funds offers a more critical outlook: "VCs are what I call 'over-boarded.' They're on like 10 or 12 boards. How can they get into any depth in any of these companies? The vision I had of them is they're sitting at a board meeting with a really clear desk—because they don't have a lot of data, they don't have a lot of contacts [with the company]. And the desk just has two buttons. One button they can hit is 'give them more money.' The other button they can hit is 'fire an executive.' And their hand is hovering between these two buttons." After working at more than a dozen companies in his 30-year career, he has come to believe VCs often base decisions on gut feelings rather than on facts or data.[51]

PORTFOLIO DIAPER CHANGING

When Brendan Richardson, a VC and professor, teaches venture capital investing courses, he shares the reality of VC life with his students. In some ways, he says, it's like observing children at play, "watching them run around, pull their pants down, poke each other, cry, scream, pull hair." The VC's job is "trying to pick, based on that information, the next Nobel Laureate or the next Super Bowl–winning quarterback." VCs know that both their own money and that of their investors is dependent upon the success of each company they fund, so they often take an active role through ongoing involvement on the board and as an on-call advisor. "It's like raising a child," says Richardson. "It's a lot of portfolio diaper changing."

He continues, "A lot of [portfolio companies] don't succeed. A lot of them go off the rails, and you have to dive in and try and get them back on. Or if you don't think that's possible, put them out of their misery. So you're a parent from toddler age through teenage years of five, 10, 15, 20 investments, and praying that one of them becomes a Nobel laureate or president of the United States," Richardson explains. "You've got to teach them how to drive, and do all the stuff that you do with kids." An early-stage startup is not just a smaller version of a large company. In a Fortune 500 company, the "product is known, the customer is known, and now it's just creating the channels, the price points, and trying to develop the product most efficiently to go to a known customer base." A startup is an organization "designed to find a scalable business model."

FAILURE & SURVIVORSHIP BIAS:
THE TRENDS BEHIND VC INVESTMENTS

One source argued that VCs' "success is random. They get a few big hits—a Facebook, or a Sun—and suddenly they think they're really smart."[52] Good fortune notwithstanding, in the high-tech world, the startup community is dependent on the venture capitalists, who provide the money. VCs primarily aim to deliver oversized returns to their investors—so they make high-risk investments with the expectation that some will fail.

In their perpetual hunt for returns, many VCs who missed the train on yesterday's hot industry still try to catch up. As a result, VCs can develop "group think" about what should be funded at any point in time,[53] and few know that as well as Tesla Motors founder Marc Tarpenning, who has sat on both sides of the VC table over the course of his career. For example, when Tarpenning and his co-founder were trying to raise money for NuvoMedia in 1997, their efforts were obstructed by Yahoo's successful IPO just a short time earlier. "Essentially," says Tarpenning, "any proposal you gave them, no matter what it was, 'We have a new semiconductor, we have a new—whatever,' the VCs would ask, 'Can't [your idea] just be a website, because we missed out on Yahoo?'" Well-known venture capitalists told Tarpenning and his co-founder, "'We are no longer investing in any company that sells a product to a customer. That was old-school behavior.' All they were investing in were websites, because anybody who surfs by is your customer. And I would say 'Where does the transaction happen? Where is the money coming from?' And they would say, 'Ah, you just don't understand.'"

Fortunately, remembers Tarpenning, "They got over that, because they discovered that in fact, they couldn't base everything just on eyeballs and advertising. When we raised money for Tesla [in the early 2000s], it was a little easier. A car company had its own problems, but VCs realized that actually making a product that somebody wanted to buy was considered to be OK now."

Whether based on consumer products, software, or websites, venture capitalists invest significant funds in startups, but the chance of even one succeeding is extremely low. According to research by Shikhar Ghosh, a senior lecturer at Harvard Business School, about three-quarters of venture-backed firms in the United States don't return investors' capital.[54] That means that each VC better have a few huge hits in the portfolio or s/he'll soon be out of business. Similarly, the National Venture Capital Association estimates the failure rate of venture-backed businesses at 25% to 30%. Of course, there are different definitions of failure: some call it the liquidation of all assets, while others view it as failure to see a specific projected return on investment by a certain date (in which case 95% of startups fail, according to Ghosh's research).[55] Ghosh says that VCs "bury their dead very quietly," meaning "they emphasize the successes, but they don't talk about the failures at all." A bias exists toward the survivors when the dead disappear.

"There's a tendency to only think about the successful people," concurs one of my sources, who has lived in the heart of Silicon Valley for 20 years. "You don't hear the stories about my VC friend who is no longer in the VC world because the fund didn't do well."[56]

On the bright side, many believe failure for both entrepreneurs and VCs is a badge of honor, and there's even a conference in San Francisco to applaud and learn from it. FailCon's website proudly proclaims it as "a one-day conference for technology entrepreneurs, investors, developers, and designers to study their own and others' failures and prepare for success." And who said winning is everything?

THE VC PUSH TOWARD HIGH-RISK VENTURES

After incorporating his first company, Peter Herz went for nearly 18 months without funding, aside from a small amount of angel money. "And there were a few things I figured out," he says. "One is that people always wonder 'When is the money going to show up? When are we going to close a VC round?'" After he became Zen about it, the funding finally arrived.

Herz explains the "disconnect between the objectives of venture capital and entrepreneurs. . . . VCs have a portfolio of companies, and their goal is to create a grand slam home run from just one or two. They don't really have a lot of appetite to build a good company; they only want to create a great company." He explains how in his experience, VCs push each of their portfolio companies to adopt "strategies that are higher risk and have a lower probability of succeeding. But, if they do succeed, then it's a bigger win." In the drive for astronomical returns, they may inadvertently crater many of their startup portfolio companies in the process. It's important to remember that while VCs can diversify among many startups, entrepreneurs are generally in only one deal at a time.

As a result of this discrepancy of objectives, VCs forced Herz to build a different kind of company than he set forth in his original business plan—a stressful strategy switch that almost sunk the ship, and gave him stomach ulcers. The VCs' strategy in this case was "to kill the product that was actually selling, and rely entirely on this other product, which had not sold, and was probably not going to sell for many years, for some very specific technical reasons. It wasn't an awful idea," Herz remembers. "It was just highly unlikely to succeed in the timeframe. And where we had very carefully thought through what we were going to build and how we were going to build it, this new plan was not based on that kind of quality thought. Therefore, it failed . . . in a very predictable way. And then we did the recap and went back to the original business plan of the company, and that's what produced the [successful] outcome," Herz says of his eventual $150 million exit.

Is the tendency to look backward at hot trends and to seek up-and-coming companies in that space a conservative characteristic? "It's a human trait," says one source.[57] Chasing investment returns is a behavioral finance trap for many retail investors, too.

Importance of Advice/Assistance Provided by Company Investors for Founders of Venture-Backed Businesses

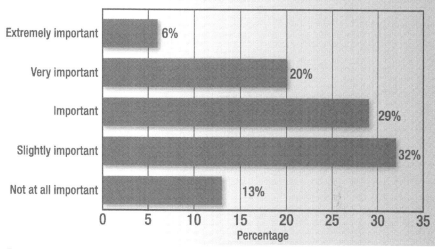

Figure 3. The importance of advice and assistance provided by company investors for founders of venture-backed businesses, as ranked by 549 entrepreneurs in the Kauffman Foundation report. (Wadhwa et al.; *The Anatomy of an Entrepreneur: Making of a Successful Entrepreneur.*)

A Kauffman Foundation study discovered that founders who received venture funding viewed investor advice more favorably than did those who received no funding.[58] Of venture-backed companies, 55% saw advice as important, though only 6% viewed it as extremely important. Conversely, 32% saw investor advice as only slightly important, while 13% saw no importance at all.

Top Five Topics to Raise When Negotiating with VCs

Before you take cash from a deep-pocketed outsider, it's best to plan for a variety of outcomes to ensure maximum financial success. Startup attorney Michael Irvine, a partner at Gunderson Dettmer, lists the top five subjects for startup founders to negotiate with VCs:

❶ **Valuation.** Determine what percentage of equity the VCs get, and how much dilution the founders get.

❷ **Liquidation preference and participation.** Understand the VC's stock ownership and how it impacts your stock in terms of when you are in or out of the money.

❸ Voting/veto blocking rights. Specifically, who has what decision-making authority over the company.

❹ Restrictions on transfer and rights of first refusal. This is an evolving area that deals with limiting transfers of stock by founders before a liquidity event.

❺ Who controls the board of directors.

The takeaway is to make sure you see eye to eye with the VCs before you sell a piece of your company—especially if they will have a large voting influence on your startup as you move into Phase 2 and beyond.

FINANCIAL PLANNING AND TAX TIPS

TIP 1 Equity Awards

Understanding your equity award inventory, and how each grant is taxed, can save you money and increase your wealth. To help demystify the process, below are some key terms. Throughout this book, I use the term "equity awards" to refer to stock options or restricted stock.

> **Incentive Stock Options (ISOs)**—Upon grant date, there are generally no tax consequences. Upon exercise, you do not recognize taxable income for regular tax purposes. However, the spread between the fair market value (FMV) on the date of exercise and the stock purchase price (the "bargain element") is taxable for alternative minimum tax (AMT) purposes. You must hold the stock for two years from the date of the grant and one year from the date of exercise to have a qualifying disposition. A gain on the sale of ISOs in a qualifying disposition is taxed at the favorable long-term capital gain rates. If you fail to meet the two holding period tests (two years from grant date and one year from exercise date), the amount by which the FMV on the date of exercise exceeds the strike price is treated as ordinary income, or compensation income, in the year that you dispose of the stock. Additional rules apply for disqualified dispositions of stock at amounts less than the FMV on the date of exercise and for disqualified dispositions that straddle two tax years.

> **Non-Qualified Stock Options (NQSOs)**—Upon grant date, generally there are no tax consequences. Upon exercise, you recognize ordinary income (generally subject to payroll taxes or self-employment taxes) to the extent that the FMV of stock on the date of exercise exceeds the strike price.

> **Employee Stock Purchase Plan (ESPP)**—If a company offers an employee discount, employees pay tax at ordinary income tax rates on the discount amount when shares are purchased, and capital gain upon the sale of the shares. The amount of the employee discount, or the difference between the price paid and the fair market value on

the date of purchase, will be included on your W-2 if you're a public company employee. When you sell the shares, the capital gain may be taxed at the lower long-term capital gain rate, depending upon how long you held the shares. A common mistake made after selling ESPP shares occurs when the sale is reported on your tax return: remember to add the employee discount amount that was included in your W-2 to the amount paid for the stock when calculating cost basis and gain.

> **Grant Date**—The date that an employee receives an equity award, such as stock options or restricted stock.

> **Vest Date**—The date the restrictions on stock options (generally based on time worked for a company) lapse, and the option to purchase stock no longer has a time- or performance-based restriction. Usually, vested shares are available for exercise and restricted stock becomes available for sale. However, specific company plans may allow for early exercise (subject to forfeiture if the shares are not vested), or may place additional restrictions on the stock. For example, a private company may not let restricted stock be sold until a change of control or an IPO.

> **Exercise Date**—The date when you elect to convert the options into actual shares of company stock by purchasing the shares at the predetermined price as set forth when granted.

> **Cashless Exercise**—An immediate sale of enough shares to pay the price of exercising the options, plus taxes, if applicable. Payroll, federal, and state taxes will usually be withheld, unless ISOs are exercised, in which case no withholding is taken.

> **Qualifying Dispositions (for ISOs)**—You must hold the stock two years from the date of the grant, and one year from the date of exercise. A qualifying disposition, where the stock is sold for more than the purchase price, is taxed favorably as a long-term capital gain.

> **Disqualifying Dispositions (for ISOs)**—If you fail to hold the stock for two years from grant date and one year from exercise date, the amount by which the fair market value on the date of exercise exceeds the strike price is treated as ordinary compensation income in the year

that you disposed of the stock. It should be included on the W-2 form you get from your company and the sale will not be subject to payroll taxes, such as FICA and Medicare. Special rules apply for stock sold at less than FMV at exercise and for exercise/sale transactions that straddle two tax years.

> **Restricted Stock Awards and Restricted Stock Units**—If you are granted restricted stock awards (RSAs) or restricted stock units (RSUs), there are no tax consequences at grant date. Upon vesting (or lapse of other restrictions), you receive shares of company stock. These shares are taxed at your ordinary income tax rate based on the value of the shares received. It's more common for larger companies than startups to issue RSUs or RSAs than stock options.

Your grant price (the value on the day you receive the restricted stock award) is irrelevant with this type of award. If you're not in a blackout period, you can sell the stock immediately upon receiving it. It acts like an ongoing bonus, as you stay with the company and vest, you receive a reward based on the current stock price. The day your stock vests, you receive taxable compensation based upon the fair market value of the shares, and your employer withholds taxes. The prudent move is usually to sell immediately; as you remain with the company, you'll continue to receive and vest in more shares.

> **Strike Price/Exercise Price**—This is the price paid when you exercise an option.

TIP 2 Early Exercise / 83(b) Election

As long as your company's plan allows it, you may exercise your options before they are vested. (The shares are still generally subject to vesting even though exercised.) By making a special election with the Internal Revenue Service, you can elect to pay tax on the bargain element at the early exercise date rather than later when you exercise the shares after they have vested. An 83(b) election is done to start the clock ticking for long-term capital gains. Special rules apply for ISOs, which should be considered before making an 83(b) election to early exercise. To get the favorable long-term capital gain tax rate applied to a gain on stock sales, you must hold the (exercised ISO) shares for at least two years from grant date and one year from exercise date. The early exercise of an ISO does not constitute an exercise for regular tax purposes, and the holding period for regular tax purposes does not start until the option would have otherwise vested. See the more comprehensive section on the pros and cons of early exercising your options on page 54.

TIP 3   Mortgages for Buying and Remodeling a Home

Generally, you can deduct all of the interest you pay on a home mortgage, up to $1.1 million, as long as the funds were used to buy, build, or maintain your primary or second home. If you already own a home that you wish to remodel, a home equity line of credit (HELOC) may be used to pay for your renovations. The interest on the HELOC is 100% deductible, as long as the HELOC and primary mortgage together don't total more than $1.1 million and the loans were used to buy, build, or maintain the property. Any interest paid on the portion of the loans over $1.1 million is not tax deductible. Beware that if you pay cash for a remodel (or for a home, for that matter), you can't later take out a loan and deduct the interest, since "non-acquisition indebtedness" is not tax deductible.

TIP 4   Alternative Minimum Tax (AMT) Basics

The AMT is a tax system that runs parallel to the regular tax system for every United States taxpayer. Created in the 1980s, the goal of AMT is to limit the amount of tax deductions generally available to high-income taxpayers. There are two AMT tax rates: 26% and 28%. IRS Form 6251 calculates the AMT. When your tentative minimum tax exceeds your regular tax, you'll pay AMT tax (the excess of tentative minimum tax over regular tax). Exercising incentive stock options can trigger AMT, and it is just one of many types of adjustments to regular tax liability used to calculate AMT. Each U.S. taxpayer pays the higher of regular tax or AMT each year. In some situations, you can get an AMT credit to use to reduce your regular tax liability in a later year.[59] The AMT credit is a complex topic beyond the scope of this book.

TIP 5   Capital Gain

Capital gain occurs when a capital asset, such as stock or a mutual fund, is sold. Gain is the amount by which the sales proceeds exceed the asset's adjusted cost basis. Lower federal income tax rates are applied to long-term capital gains, defined as assets you've held for more than one year.

TIP 6   Stock Option Planning

Whether you have Incentive Stock Options (ISOs) or Non-Qualified Stock Options (NQSOs), many tax planning strategies are available to you. Since there are many nuances to stock option planning, a complete understanding and assessment of your specific circumstances should be undertaken, preferably with a tax professional, before you take any action with your options.

> **ISOs** require consideration of the following factors:

- Your marginal income tax rate on ordinary income versus the income tax rate on long-term capital gains. Generally, capital gains will be taxed at a lower rate than your ordinary income.
- The relationship between the exercise price of the option and the stock price on the day you exercise.
- Whether exercising ISOs will push you into AMT.
- The date you exercise (to determine when you must pay any taxes due).
- Whether you are required to make estimated tax payments.
- A realistic expectation for the price of the stock 12 months and one day after exercise. If the stock price is lower a year from the exercise date, it may make more sense to exercise and immediately sell the stock today and pay more tax than to hold on for a year hoping the stock price will go up. Examples abound (such as Groupon[60] and Zynga[61]) in which this buy-and-hold strategy did not work out for option holders who exercised but did not sell quickly, because the stock price dropped significantly after the IPO. Note that unless you are selling on the private market, you cannot sell company stock until Phase 3, after the company has gone public.

> **Non-qualified stock options** provide tax planning opportunities, too. Some important issues to consider are:

- Whether you have the cash to exercise the options.
- Your investment portfolio diversification. (If you hold a lot of company stock, your concentrated position is a risky venture, although you may not be able to sell much, if any, stock until Phase 3.)
- Your cash flow needs.
- Whether you must make estimated tax payments.
- Nonfinancial factors, such as how long you plan to remain at the company, and when you expect to retire.
- Your guess about the price of the stock at the end of 12 months and one day after exercise.
- Whether you have capital loss carryovers, which can be used to offset gain from stock sales dollar for dollar.
- In years of low income, exercising options is a way to generate additional taxable income to preserve itemized deductions that may otherwise be lost.

Before your liquidity event, consult with an accountant on the personal financial impact of taking action with equity awards. Multiyear tax planning includes pushing income to otherwise low-income years, taking deductions in high tax years or using charitable planning strategies in conjunction with stock sales to reduce your taxes.

TIP 7   Section 83(b) Election to Early Exercise Options

Some companies offer equity compensation through stock grants. For early employees, using the 83(b) election can start the clock on long-term capital gains (page 53). It's best to make an 83(b) election on stock options when the spread between the exercise price and the fair market value is low. To understand what a Section 83(b) election is and how and when you might use it, it's a good idea to familiarize yourself with a few key terms.

When you have equity awards subject to forfeiture, they will usually be on a vesting schedule. Know when your shares vest and strategize when to exercise them. When your equity awards vest, you have the right to exercise them. A common vesting schedule is 25% of your options vest every year for four years. When your options vest, think about when you want to exercise them. Exercise means that you actually purchase the stock at the grant price or strike price.

Stock options and stock are not the same thing. Stock options give you the right to buy shares at a predetermined price. For example, the company might give you the option to buy 10,000 shares for $0.50 per share. Later, the fair market value may be $10 per share. You don't actually have any ownership in the company—those 10,000 shares—until you exercise the options and buy the stock at the grant price or strike price. (If your strike price is $.50, you pay 50 cents per share to exercise the options.)

Generally, with non-qualified stock options you don't report any income until the exercise date, at which time you pay tax (at your ordinary income tax rate) on the difference between what you paid for the stock and the fair market value on the date of exercise. If the fair market value is much higher when the options vest than when you were granted them, you could be looking at a large tax payment as a result of exercising shares. (The rules for incentive stock options are slightly different: Upon exercise, you may pay AMT, but not ordinary income; upon the sale, you may be able to use the AMT credit to offset regular income.)

A Section 83(b) election gives you the option to exercise early (before your options vest) to reduce the amount of taxes you have to pay. The early exercise allows you to purchase the shares prior to vesting, usually while the stock price is still relatively low. This way, you can presumably reduce the spread between your purchase price and the fair market value of the stock on the day you buy it. If you decide to participate in an 83(b) election, then you must file a statement with the IRS no later than 30 days after the date the property was transferred.[62] According to Kaye A. Thomas, author of *Consider Your Options*, failing to meet that 30-day deadline is the biggest problem with the Section 83(b) election. Thomas warns, "You can't wait to file your tax return to make this election. You have to do it right away."

Most advisors agree that if you think your company's stock price will increase, and your exercise price is low, you should consider exercising early because of the relatively low up-front cost and long-run tax benefits. Making an 83(b) election is a risky move, since the stock price could go down while you hold on to the shares. And, if you later forfeit the stock (voluntarily or not) after making the election, you cannot claim a deduction.[63]

> **Examples of the Section 83(b) Election**

Consider the following scenario:

- Say you were given a non-qualified option to buy 50,000 shares at $0.30 per share soon after a company started, and you are very optimistic about its future. The stock price is currently valued at $2 and there is talk that it will increase to $7 if your upcoming financing round goes well. If the company can successfully IPO in two years as planned, then, colleagues are telling you, the price might increase to $25 per share. If you sell all your shares at $25 per share, you would have a profit of $1,235,000 before taxes!

- The difference between the exercise price and the fair market value on the date of exercise is considered compensation income, taxable at your ordinary income tax rate. Any subsequent appreciation of the stock between when you purchased it and when you sell it is taxed at the more favorable capital gain tax rates, as long as you've held the shares for at least one year. A long-term capital gain rate of 20% is used in the examples that follow. However, the federal long-term capital gain tax rate is currently 23.8% for those in the highest tax bracket.

> **Example A: No Early Exercise, Sell Stock at $25 per Share**

- If you exercise your options when the fair market value is $25, the difference between the exercise price and the grant price ($25 – $0.30) gives you $24.70 per share of compensation income. This is "ordinary" income, taxed at your marginal tax bracket. If you're in the 40% tax bracket, your tax liability on the transaction would be $494,000. If you were to wait a year and a day from your exercise before selling, you could qualify for the long-term capital gain rate—the "promised land," as one interviewee called it—on the appreciation beyond what you purchased the stock for and what you sold it for. (Bear in mind that waiting another year after the IPO or liquidity event is always risky.)

Exercise Price = $15,000 ($0.30 x 50,000 shares)

Tax on Exercise = $494,000
($25 – $0.30 = $24.70 x 50,000 shares = $1,235,000 x 40%)

Sales Price (on day of exercise) = $1,250,000 ($25 x 50,000 shares)

Net After-Tax Proceeds from Sale = $741,000
($1,250,000 – $15,000 – $494,000)

Note: There's no tax on the sales price, because the sales price is equal to the fair market value on the date of exercise.

> **Example B: Early Exercise via 83(b) Election, Sell at $25 per Share**
Contrast Example A with an early exercise via an 83(b) election. You purchase the shares for $0.30 each, when the market value is $0.30. The spread between the price you paid and the market value is $0 per share on 50,000 shares, meaning no appreciation is taxed as compensation income. The example below assumes you are in the 40% ordinary income tax bracket.

- If the share price rises as expected, any future gain beyond the exercise price of $0.30 per share is taxed at the lower capital gain tax rate, assuming you hold for at least one year. (The equation gets trickier if you're in a high tax bracket when you exercise and a lower tax bracket when you sell. Note that you may also be taxed if there's been appreciation in the stock between the grant date and the exercise date. A multiyear tax projection would be very helpful.)

Exercise Price = $15,000 ($0.30 x 50,000 shares)

Tax on Exercise = $0

Sales Price (two years after exercise) = $1,250,000
($25 x 50,000 shares)

Tax on Sale = $247,000
($25 – $0.30 = $24.70 x 50,000 shares = $1,235,000 x 20%)

Net After-Tax Proceeds from Sale = $988,000
($1,250,000 – $15,000 – $247,000)

In the above examples, the increase in after-tax sales proceeds from an early exercise would be $247,000. As you can see, with a smaller spread between exercise price and market value on the date of exercise, your risk from an early exercise is smaller, since you are paying less tax on the exercise.

> **Risks of an 83(b) Election**

In interviews with people who lived through the dot-com era, I heard over and over about tech employees who didn't take advantage of low-priced stock through an 83(b) election. Describing the late '90s tech boom, this quote by a C-level executive echoes many: "One executive who didn't exercise his options early [he did not file an 83(b) election], exercised them after the company went public. He then had tax issues, and the stock went way down. He took a loan out to exercise the stock as well, to pay for the taxes, and the stock went way, way down. So he had the worst of all worlds: high taxes, and he couldn't sell his stock. It was as dumb as all get-out. [This was] an executive at a major, major company that rode the wave up, and then rode the wave down."[64]

In the examples above, I assumed that the stock's value was increasing, which is what created the tax savings. If the company's stock price drops after you exercise, then it's possible that you will end up paying too much tax.

Jason Graham, a CPA and tax advisor, told stories of how some of his pre-IPO clients got caught in this trap. For example, he consulted with a pre-IPO company whose internal valuation lost almost half of its value by the time it went IPO.[65] "Based upon how other similar companies have fared post-IPO, a number of the individuals at this company felt quite confident that a post-IPO price per share has got to be higher," Graham explained. "So they're thinking, it could be 1.5X, it could be 2X, it could be 3X. They were very bullish about where the company was going to go. And they had reasons for feeling that way. They felt like they kind of had a corner on that particular market that they developed, they had a name for themselves, they had one successful venture after another, and that would continue."[66]

So some, filled with optimism about the company's future, exercised at a "healthy" price per share with a very low strike price, facing a significant tax bill with the hope that the fair market value would increase after the IPO. Graham encourages his clients working at startups to think about the downside possibilities of their action (or inaction) with stock options.

When it came time to determine what they could afford to exercise, some of the employees decided they would cover the taxes by selling their shares. The S-1 had been filed, so they assumed there would be enough time for the company to go public and their six-month lockup period to end before tax season. "I knew it was going to be a little tight," Graham remembers, "because I remember having conversations with them saying, 'You're going to need cash by April 15. So the hope was we can go public before October 15, so the six-month lockup comes off before April 15.' Well, that didn't happen. They were hoping it would, but I remember some delay in the IPO due to market volatility and timing, but then eventually it went public toward the end of the year."

Those employees managed to "scrape and borrow to get the taxes paid," but that was not the end of their troubles. "I would never have anticipated [the stock price] being so volatile so fast. You think about, in exactly one year's time, the stock dropped in value by 40% from its pre-IPO internal valuation to its opening price at IPO, while it was public it went up 40% from the opening price, but now [in mid-2012 it] is trading at less than 20% of its internal pre-IPO valuation, all within one year. That's a lot of up and down, a lot of volatility in one year," recalls Graham. "There's no predictability to it, there's no rhyme or reason to it." After our 2012 interview, the stock price fell even further. According to Graham, at that time most of the employees held their stock when it was trading at lower values, hoping it would recover to justify the high taxes incurred from the exercise.

This situation also brings to light another issue involved with participating in a Section 83(b) election: how to afford the up-front cost to exercise. Graham recommends his clients who are bullish on the stock borrow the cash to pay the taxes, insisting that "if they can do an early exercise, exercise all of [their options]." A tax payment on the spread when the stock price is low could make a substantial difference in the net sales proceeds later on. Many, he says, turn to family and friends for the cash. Before Oracle went public in 1986, CFO Roy Bukstein borrowed $4,000 from his dad to buy his pre-IPO shares. He encourages others who believe in the future of their company to borrow money to early exercise stock options.

Other pitfalls include the opportunity cost of paying the tax earlier rather than later and the restrictions placed on the options (such as losing the options if you leave the company). If you are new to options, then it is best to discuss your situation with a tax advisor before making a decision to participate in a Section 83(b) election. The rules for making the election are very specific, including the requirement of filing the election with the IRS and with your company within 30 days.[67]

> How to Make the 83(b) Election

Here are the requirements for an individual making an 83(b) election to early exercise equity awards:

1. Send a copy of the election to the IRS within 30 days of receiving the property (stock or options).

2. Provide a copy of the election to your employer.

3. Attach a copy of the election to your tax return for the year the election is made.

4. On your tax return, include the fair market value of the property received (less any amount paid for it) as compensation income; your employer should have added the amount to your W-2.

Taxpayers who receive stock with restrictions through the exercise of ISOs may be able to eliminate the AMT consequences by making an 83(b) election. The election in the case of ISOs simply increases the amount recognized for AMT purposes, allowing taxpayers to lock in the AMT consequences rather than waiting until the stock is vested.[68]

To protect yourself and avoid unnecessary correspondence with the Internal Revenue Service, it's best to follow these five steps:

1. Complete the Section 83(b) election form provided by your employer. If you are married, have your spouse sign the election, too.

2. Prepare a cover letter to the Internal Revenue Service (IRS).

3. Send the cover letter with the originally executed Section 83(b) election form along with one copy of the form and a self-addressed stamped envelope so that the IRS may return a date-stamped copy of the Section 83(b) election to you.

4. Mail the materials via certified mail, return receipt requested, to the Internal Revenue Service at the IRS address where you file your personal income tax returns. Have the package date-stamped at the post office, and retain the certified receipt that includes a dated postmark.

5. Retain the IRS file-stamped copy along with the mail confirmations from the post office for your records for four years after the shares the 83(b) election relates to are sold.

Checklist for Startup Founders in Phase 1

Review the items below before and during Phase 1 to optimize your personal financial wealth.

CORPORATE ISSUES

❑ Draft your long-term vision for the company. Do you want a small business run by a close team, or do you want to be a large public company?

❑ Hire an experienced startup attorney early on to set up corporate documents, founders' agreements, and vesting schedules for stock options. Determine equity ownership and ownership of the company's IP.

❑ Understand the ideal entity structure for your company and what will happen in the event of a change in control; it's hard to argue that you have a great vision for the company if you're still holding on to all the rights and intellectual property (IP).

❑ Decide who will serve as your corporate officers and who will sit on the board of directors.

❑ Settle valuation. The temptation is to price the company low, since a low stock price means founders and early employees pay little or nothing for their stock. But the IRS can step in and recalculate the early valuation at a higher value, potentially causing unwanted tax consequences. It's best to have a 409A valuation done within the first year of a startup's existence. (In practice, a 409A valuation usually occurs after a significant financing event or increase in sales.) Ideally, you will do these annually if you expect to raise VC funds. There's a "safe harbor" under 409A if you do valuations, whereby the IRS can't revalue the company later on.

❑ Determine whether Series FF stock should be written into the company's charter to provide founders with early liquidity.

❑ Hire an accountant to prepare pro-forma financial statements.

❑ Have a CPA prepare a business tax projection so that you can reserve cash for taxes and avoid surprises later on.

❏ If you plan to get outside funding for your company via banks or investors, you'll need a personal financial statement. Scrutinize your personal and business financial statements before going to investors.

PERSONAL ISSUES

❏ Prepare a personal cash flow projection for at least two to three years, to understand the commitment you will make to the startup.

❏ Prepare an inventory of your stock, options, and other equity awards. Include the vesting schedule for each award. Understanding how your equity awards work will help you maximize your wealth.

❏ Consider making an 83(b) election, if your company allows employees to make this election on unvested stock options or restricted stock. If so, and there's a low cost to exercise your options and a low "spread," determine how much cash you'll need for both the exercise and the tax bill.

❏ If you are early exercising stock options, consider hiring an accountant for personal tax and cash flow planning.

❏ Increase your knowledge, via classes or books, about functional areas of the company beyond your skills and existing knowledge.

❏ If you have the inclination for self-improvement, find a coach to provide nonfinancial insight about your strengths and weaknesses, and solutions for stronger business skills.

❏ Join an entrepreneurs' group to share business advice and support with like-minded peers.

Phase 1 can last anywhere from two to 40 years. If your company has stalled in this phase, your personal finances can't support your needs, and funding options don't seem to be fast approaching, consider jumping off the Entrepreneur's Wheel here. Otherwise, continue on to Phase 2.

PHASE 2
RAMPING UP

Pre-Transition Phase
0–24 Months

The Entrepreneur's Wheel of Life℠

Pre-Transition Phase
2–40 years

1 Laying the Foundation

Challenges

QUALITY OF LIFE
- Preoccupation with startup
- Optimism
- Loneliness
- Improvisation
- Tenacity

FINANCIAL
- Raising capital
- Below-market salary
- Accountability to investors
- Funneling all resources into the company

Most entrepreneurs never retire.

They just keep going back to Phase 1.

Post-Transition Phase
1–24 months

3 Realizing the Dream

Challenges

QUALITY OF LIFE
- Figuring out what's next
- Determining how to return to Phase 1

FINANCIAL
- Accountability to shareholders, board, and management
- Increasing enterprise value
- Strategizing goals with financial resources
- Expensive purchases (home, car, jewelry, boat)

Pre-Transition Phase
0–24 months

2 Ramping Up

Challenges

QUALITY OF LIFE
- Maintaining balance while working long hours
- Excitement
- Persistence

FINANCIAL
- Negotiations
- Increasing enterprise value
- Compensation
- Learning new business skills
- Financial and tax planning
- Accountability to investors and board

LIQUIDITY EVENT

COMMON TO ALL PHASES

Challenge	Concerns	Solutions
Maximize Value of Equity Awards (ISO, NQ, RSA, RSU, ESPP)	Wealth Preservation Tax Reduction Wealth Protection Passing Assets to Heirs Charitable Giving	Financial Education Expert Team of Advisors Personal CFO

RAMPING UP

SALES ARE CONTINUING THEIR UPWARD TRAJECTORY. You are preparing for a liquidity event that could be an acquisition, merger, or IPO.

In her work at the Kauffman Foundation, Lesa Mitchell has become well acquainted with thousands of stressed entrepreneurs' "huge highs and lows" throughout the process of building a company: "[They say] 'I think I'm going to be out of business, and then I get a customer. Then, my system shuts down and I'm going to be out of business, and then I get an investor'. . . . It is a serious problem in the first five years."[1]

In Phase 1, it's all about perseverance as you stay optimistic about your ideas and begin to search for more cash to keep your operations running. Because "solving problems is a different skill set than creating a product,"[2] be prepared to face new challenges as your company prepares for a liquidity event. For example, the VCs might replace your CEO with a more experienced CEO, who may, claims Peter Herz, be "playing for the VC firm, because that's where they're going to get their next gig," rather than looking out for the best interest of the company. This is problematic for an unsuspecting startup. Or, as in the sad story of the founders of Dragon speech recognition software (see page 73), having investment bankers whose incentives clash with yours could cause you to lose both your company and your wealth.

In order to protect yourself as you ramp up from Phase 2 toward your event, do your due diligence (i.e., kick-the-tires-type research) on executives introduced by your VC, attorneys, and investment bankers; prepare for surprises in the final moments before the deal; address your tax and financial planning opportunities with a trustworthy accountant or financial planner before the deal is inked; understand equity awards and consider early exercising; and maintain positive team dynamics in the midst of all the changes.

Questions from a Former Dealmaker

When you enter into discussions with potential investors or acquirers, you'll want to prepare for a variety of possible outcomes. As someone who negotiated and structured many deals as an analyst at JPMorgan and later in corporate development at Yahoo, Sylvia Yam advises entrepreneurs to ask themselves the following questions:

- What do you want for your company?
- What do you want to happen to your product?
- What do you want for your team? You've invested in your employees, and they've invested in you for many years. They're like family. Do you want this to be their outcome? How much control do you want over that?
- What do you want for your future?
- If you're contemplating an acquisition, put thought into the acquiring company. As your future employer, does this move fulfill your career goals?

Only after pondering these questions, Yam says, are you prepared to negotiate with the acquirer. A good deal means different things to different people, so be sure to understand your ultimate goals.

THE DEALMAKER EXTRAORDINAIRE
FROM ENGINEER TO ENTREPRENEUR TO VENTURE CAPITALIST.

One serial engineer and entrepreneur I spoke with requested anonymity because many of the tales and anecdotes he shared were under nondisclosure agreements.[3] But he did want to share his story. His multifaceted career has given him a deep and nuanced understanding of the high-tech world. In addition to his intellectual aptitude, his professional impact stems from his ability to rally a team and his varied experience as a company founder and executive before, during, and after the dot-com boom.

He started his career as an engineer at a well-known information technology company before joining the early team at what would become a hot dot-com company. He recalls: "I did everything from training, to writing code, to traveling around the world and helping customers." He then co-founded a company that went public during the dot-com heyday. Currently, he's an executive at a midsized tech company.

Like many successful company founders, the engineer and entrepreneur briefly became a technology investor for an investment bank. However, while he acknowledges that some entrepreneurs enjoy finance, "I decided that venture capital wasn't for me. I went off back into my heart of hearts, which is being an engineer." He believes Phases 1 and 2 are all about enjoying the work, so he stays in Phase 3 for as little time as possible, then immediately jumps back to Phase 1 to start or join a new venture with a dedicated team.

Holding the Deal Ransom: Brace Yourself for Business Negotiations

The goal of Phase 2 is all about "transitioning to the liquidity event," says the engineer and entrepreneur. Right before the event there will be a "tidying up of the business or pinning down all the loose ends. Every liquidity event that I've ever been involved in, there comes a moment where people have to buy off." And someone will have to sacrifice for the greater good of the others. Issues can range from a particular clause in an employment contract or a developer's patent, to a transferability issue or a share valuation issue for the buyout or conversion.

On top of that, every single deal he has seen has involved a surprise crisis "that potentially will kill the liquidity event hours before it's supposed to happen." From a wind-down to a sale, then, you should always expect surprises: "Generally speaking," he says, "it's the CEO of the company who is the main lynchpin in this negotiation, because he wants to get the deal done on behalf of the shareholders. And he's trying to remove impediments to get there."

Since the deal and your potential wealth have many opportunities to disintegrate in the final hours before you get paid, it is risky to spend any of your expected windfall before the deal goes through. As this engineer and entrepreneur advises, "Know that you have to have the gravitas or disposition to say, 'Okay I've expected this, and I think I'll punch it in the gut.' If you brace for it, you nail it. If you don't brace for it, it's going to hurt."

Below are some examples of last-minute surprises seed investors, employees, and co-founders can bring up late in Phase 2—generally in the month before the liquidity event—that require tough conversations and intense last-minute negotiations.

- "The person in the company that has a change-of-control clause in their contract. And guess what? The deal's not going to get done if they keep their change of control.
- "The person whose stock might be underwater, but it's the right thing to do for the company to liquidate at that rate. But they're not going to vote for it, so you've got to get them past that.
- "The early investor who feels that you should hold off on an acquisition," and instead go public at a later time.
- "The five employees that realize their stock isn't going to be worth what they thought it was going to be worth, and they want to vote against [the liquidity event].

- "One of the early guys who was in the company decides that one of the patents he had signed over to the corporation wasn't signed over properly. There was some sort of patent transfer that hadn't quite executed according to his lawyer. So he was going to say, 'You can't take the IP [intellectual property] unless you buy me off for XYZ price,'" remembers the engineer and entrepreneur. The team negotiated, and he probably got more than he deserved, but the deal went through.

While he claims to have mellowed with age, he is a natural peacemaker and a great team player. As a CEO or entrepreneur, his last-minute team negotiations sometimes come down to a straight-shooting conversation, acknowledging the team members' years of work for the company and the existing contract terms, while stressing the need for a personal sacrifice. According to the engineer and entrepreneur, those conversations go something like this: "We have two ways to do this. You can scuttle the whole deal, and everyone around here will basically not be rewarded. Or you can give up on this benefit for yourself, and for the greater good get this deal done. What do you want to do?"

Ultimately, business success is all about the team: "Great teams can take average products and make huge markets out of them," he says. "And poor teams can take great products and destroy them. So, if you can find the right team and you can find the right folks, then you can generally make the negotiations easier. But it always comes down to greed and fear, too."

When Should a Banker Be Part of Your Deal?

Although Phases 1 and 2 are busy times when it can be hard to step away from work to plan for your financial future, entrepreneurs like James and Janet Baker (see the Dragon Systems sidebar on page 73), who didn't get the help they expected from investment bankers, would have been wise to read this chapter.

An investment banker's fee means an extra layer of cost, but at the same time, in some situations an "i-banker" translates to a higher selling price for the founders. I-bankers can be good matchmakers if you're looking for an acquirer to purchase your company. You'll also need an i-banker if your company is going public.

The complexity of the deal matters in your decision, but a good rule of thumb for when to involve a banker is a sale price of at least $10 to $30 million, says Mitch Cohen, a retired private equity investor who has been involved in many M&A deals.[4] If the acquiring company has a banker, you may need a banker. "You want principals to talk to principals, lawyers to talk to lawyers," but lawyers should not talk to investment bankers because "it's a weird dynamic," advises Cohen.

After working with another investment bank to raise growth capital for NeighborCity, Jonathan Cardella now understands that he was just one of the bank's many clients. He offers this advice to entrepreneurs who hire bankers: "If you can't get through the noise, you're toast. I feel like a lot of i-banks, when the deal isn't big enough, [send] a blast communication that isn't necessarily that effective. Even when they do call [a potential partner or acquirer], they're contractors, so you don't really know what that call ever was or who made it. Associates staff what partners consider to be the 'grunt work' but that you [as an entrepreneur] consider 'make-or-break' work. You don't really know how they did or what they did. You're just taking what they tell you at face value. And I think that's a really dangerous thing to do when you're dealing with an asset of credible value."

If he were looking to sell a company in the future, and the deal were worth less than $100 million, Cardella says he would build his own materials and target list rather than hire an investment banker. An M&A attorney would likely be on Cardella's team, regardless of whether bankers were involved. Cardella is more of a do-it-yourselfer than most entrepreneurs when it comes to his business.

If you choose Cardella's route and use a lawyer for the negotiations rather than an i-banker, make sure your attorney is business savvy and has actually negotiated deals before. Many lawyers sit in offices drafting documents all day long but have never actually sat across from a negotiator with opposing interests. In some cases, then, former private equity dealmaker Cohen argues, "An entrepreneurial lawyer . . . can be more valuable than a banker. People tend to hire a banker because they've got a good reputation."

Unfortunately, Cohen says, many people don't do the due diligence on the investment bank before hiring, due to time constraints to complete the deal or competing time commitments within the company. The dollars are big, and the stakes are enormous for your company and your personal financial future. It's important to understand what you're getting into before you sign a contract. Due diligence is "real work," says Cohen, "like you would do if you hired an employee," which includes:

- Asking who or which team will work on your deal.
- Calling references to discuss their experiences with your potential future team.

As anyone who outsources can attest, once you get over the due diligence hurdle (such as researching and interviewing an advisor who you feel could be a good fit), the value from a professional advisor can often be greater than what you can get on your own. Certainly, they will save you time. The key is to find the banker or advisor who will serve your best interest.

CASE STUDY
THE DRAGON SYSTEMS DEAL: POOR ADVICE AND TRAGIC LOSS

FOUNDERS SOLD 400-PERSON COMPANY BUT WALKED AWAY WITH NOTHING DUE TO A FAILURE OF DUE DILIGENCE.

> If you've seen the heartwarming ads on television in which a blogger's spoken thoughts are automatically typed up, a teenage boy vocally updates his Facebook status, and a poor typist, whose Italian immigrant parents couldn't write, can now speak and have her family's history auto-typed, you probably think that the Bakers, the creators of Dragon voice recognition software, must be wealthy geniuses. Well, you're half-right. Both PhDs and "credited with advancing speech technology far faster than anyone thought possible," the Bakers had still not realized their creation's full potential before falling victim to

what the *New York Times* called "the business deal from hell."[5] Their story is especially sad, because in the acquisition deal gone horribly wrong, they lost not only their net worth in the company they spent decades building but also the software itself.

Passionate about accomplishing elegant speech recognition, James Baker incorporated an algorithm based on the probability that one sound followed another, rather than trying to teach the computer how to interpret accents and dialects. Over many decades, the Bakers built and refined their software products to interpret voice commands. The next step in the evolution was to build continuous dictation, but they didn't have the capital. They finally allowed Seagate, one of the world's largest manufacturers of hard disk drives, to invest $20 million in return for a 25% stake in Dragon. This capital infusion allowed their next product, Dragon NaturallySpeaking, to recognize "more words than could be found in a standard collegiate dictionary." It was available in six languages and could handle normal speech, even sentences with words that sound alike, such as "Please write a letter right now to Mrs. Wright."[6] The Bakers considered taking Dragon public, but soon offers to acquire Dragon Systems started rolling in from companies like Sony and Intel.

The Bakers wanted an advisor to guide them in managing all the incoming offers and in performing due diligence on potential acquirers. At that time, "Goldman was the alpha dog in the lucrative game of mergers and acquisitions," and the Bakers hired the investment bank known for its "ruthless professionalism" for a $5 million flat fee.[7] According to the engagement letter, Goldman was to provide "financial advice and assistance in connection with this potential transaction, which may include performing valuation analysis," as well as assistance with "negotiating the final aspects of the transaction." Though Dragon was the culmination of their long careers and, according to the *Times*, a "third child" to the Bakers, it was small potatoes to Goldman Sachs, who assigned four bankers to the deal—ages 21, 25, 32, and 42—who were later dubbed "The Goldman Four" when post-deal trouble began.

As talks with other companies stagnated, a representative from Goldman accompanied Janet Baker and Dragon's CFO to Belgium to meet with the executives of Lernout & Hauspie (L&H) who proposed a $580 million deal, half in cash, half in company stock. The Bakers weren't completely sold, as news had recently been circulating about L&H's questionable revenue growth in the Asian markets. The rumors turned out to be true.

While the Bakers were very concerned about L&H's stock price volatility, they believed, incorrectly, that Goldman's analysts had been covering L&H and would communicate any dangers to the Goldman Four team. It would have been easy for Goldman's analysts to call up the customers of L&H and check the numbers—which, unfortunately for the Bakers, their Goldman team didn't request, nor did the Goldman Four feel compelled to do themselves.

When it came time to make an agreement, no Goldman representatives attended the meeting; a few days beforehand, the Goldman contact said he would be away on vacation and couldn't make the meeting, nor would anyone else from Goldman attend. Further, the agreement was changed at that meeting, from a half-stock to an all-stock deal. And without anyone from Goldman at the meeting to advise them otherwise, the Bakers inked the deal.

One month later, the story broke that L&H had been fabricating sales data. (All it took to crack the case? A few calls to customers L&H claimed to have, who denied all sales.) The stock and everything the Bakers had to show for their life's work were worthless. "The money was one thing. But what they really wanted was the opportunity to complete the work they had started decades earlier,"[8] since the agreement also stipulated that the Bakers would work at L&H after the acquisition. On top of everything, they couldn't even reclaim their technology; it was sold at an auction after L&H went bankrupt.

It then surfaced that two years earlier, Goldman had looked closely at L&H. Goldman itself had considered investing $30 million in the company, but backed out after preliminary due diligence, which included calling the customers.

During a deposition in the lawsuit brought by the Bakers against Goldman Sachs, the Goldman Four insisted they gave the Bakers "great advice." The Goldman Four were repeatedly asked to clarify how the advice had been so good when the Bakers lost everything. The bankers' response? "We guided them to a completed transaction."[9]

Learning from the Bakers and Their Bankers: How to Negotiate a Fair Deal

What can you take away from the tragic $580 million loss of Dragon software, the life's work of James and Janet Baker? Mergers and acquisitions attorney Marlee Myers, the managing partner of the Pittsburgh office of Morgan Lewis, offers succinct advice: Hire someone like her and get the right help on the business front.[10] Via email Myers explains, "Diligence on the buyer should have been extremely important to them. They shouldn't have assumed that Goldman would do the diligence for them; this is not typically the i-banker's job." Additionally, "a seller who is being paid in stock of the buyer should not rely on their investment banker for financial and business diligence on the buyer. Of course, in a cash deal, that type of diligence isn't needed."[11]

Although the Bakers did seek outside help—the "best," or so they thought—they were missing a legal champion, or a due diligence expert,[12] and they had a compensation agreement with their banker that included a large minimum fee. What they didn't understand are the adverse motivations between client and investment banker. "Basically, an investment banker can be very helpful if you understand that they have a financial incentive to get the deal done, even if it's a bad deal for you," Myers explains. Someone who gets a large minimum fee for closing the deal, regardless of your net proceeds or goals, has little incentive to advise you to walk away. If your advisor (or banker, lawyer, or financial planner, for that matter) lacks incentive to act on your behalf, you could experience unpleasant surprises and disappointment.

A better idea in these situations is to hire a team of advisors who are working to optimize your success. For legal help, "you really need to find someone that you click with and is excellent at what they do—at the lawyer things, but also just really understands what your objectives are and how to achieve them. That's their job." Likewise, she suggests complementing legal advice with a corporate accountant or "a diligence consultant who is going to ask a lot of hard questions about the numbers and is going to do some digging if you are being paid in stock rather than cash."

Think carefully about the advisors you choose. Investment bankers "can help to negotiate the price and terms" of the deal, says Myers.[13] Yet their motivation can simply be to close the deal rather than see you achieve your goals—whether you desire more money or a specific next step in your career (in the case of a merger or acquisition). It's a good idea to have unbiased attorneys and accountants on your team whose incentives are allied with yours.

Beyond knowing your size relative to the other fish in the advisor's pond, Myers offers this final piece of advice: "You just have to understand what (bankers) do and what they don't do, what they're incented by, and what they're not. They're not incented by telling you, 'Don't do this deal.'"

Take Myers's wise words seriously. As part of your trusted team of advisors, seek out unbiased professionals who are compensated whether the deal closes or not.

Vetting Investment Bankers

Entrepreneur Rob Nail was also displeased with the first bank his company, Velocity11, hired when it was looking to be acquired.[14] "We brought in a banker to help vet the deal and make sure it was market," says Nail. He wanted to be certain that his company wasn't worth a lot more than the price the acquiring firm offered, and he was also hoping to bid up the selling price. "And that turned out to be a pretty lame process," Nail recalls. "The banker really knew that was the deal that we wanted to do, and didn't really work very hard at having a back-up plan."

While that deal ultimately fell through, the next time Nail tried to sell his company, he took a different, more successful approach with the bank. The contract with the second investment bank was based on an incentive schedule, in which the bank's compensation was related to the company's final selling price. This time around, the investment bank was an extremely positive asset to the process. It helped Velocity11 build its pitch, and then, Nail remembers, the bank was able to "create a real process, where we've got a couple groups literally bidding on the business." More importantly, Nail worked well with the bank. "I felt like we had a good dialogue with the bankers, so they were very clear, updating us, telling us what happened at every call, at every meeting." The Velocity11 team felt they were part of the negotiations, and trust came naturally, "because they were very transparent with us, and they gave us a clear understanding of what their strategy was" with each potential acquirer.

While attorney Myers cautions about the incentives that drive investment banks, she also states there are three situations in which investment banks can provide real value. The first is price discovery, in which "they can help you figure out what your business is worth" when it comes time to sell. An investment banker is also extremely valuable in connecting you to the potential network of buyers, and "if there are a lot of potential buyers, they can help you run an orderly process to sell." Finally, i-bankers "can help to negotiate the price and terms" of the deal.[15]

Many entrepreneurs see the value in hiring professional advisors for their company, but fail to adequately address their personal finances early enough.

Lessons Learned: Higher Taxes Without a Plan

Here is an example where an advisor could have helped one entrepreneur avoid significant tax dollars.

"When I look back," says serial entrepreneur Santosh Sharan, "I think I made some terrible mistakes."[16] Believing his acquisition payout was not big enough to merit much planning—"I had some different numbers in mind when I started the company," he remembers—he didn't see the benefit of tax planning. Yet paying a few thousand dollars for a professional to look at two or three years at once could have allowed him to strategize ways to shift income and/or deductions between the years and lower his tax bill.

"I am less about planning," says the engineer entrepreneur. "I make decisions spontaneously. And liquidity is not at the top of my mind. So I really wasn't trying to maximize. And yet, the reality of life is that it's stupid to not be careful or smart about money."

He tells me what he learned the hard way. His company was acquired, and he negotiated for a six-month retention during the integration period. His last day was to be November 30, after which he would take time off and earn no income while planning his next startup. On the day his company was sold, he received 80% of the sales price, in cash. On his last day at work, his restricted stock vested and he received the remaining 20%. He was already in a high tax bracket for the year from his salary. Plus, he had a gain from the sale of his company (which can minimize tax deductions). If instead of having the stock vest on November 30, he negotiated to have it vest just a month later—January 1 of the following year—he could have significantly reduced his tax bill by spreading income between two years.

"I didn't need the money," he reasoned. Yet, "I ended up with a larger tax bill." Now Sharan realizes, "I could have easily negotiated to transfer the stock vesting to the next year. All I had to do was stay or negotiate a longer retention."

If you're in talks to sell your company, a tax projection before the deal is finalized could prevent you from paying tens or even hundreds of thousands of dollars more than you need to.

Don't Put Your Personal Finances at Risk by Spending Future Wealth

The water coolers of Silicon Valley are rife with tales of paper millionaires who didn't diversify, spent money they didn't actually have, and wound up with nothing. In the dot-com heyday, remembers Marc Tarpenning, both founders and employees "assumed their paper wealth was real wealth, and it's all concentrated in one stock. . . . They had these options, and they're suddenly worth tens of millions of dollars, and . . . they didn't want to exercise and take [their wealth off the table], because it's only going to go up. So they would instead borrow lots of money and build a giant house. And then, of course, they lost the house and everything." Tarpenning gives the example of Pets.com: when the company went public with an insane valuation, the founders and executives "borrowed against their shares and bought giant houses in Atherton and Burlingame, and [other] fancy neighborhoods, and then of course, by the time they could sell the shares, they were worth one hundredth or one thousandth of what they thought they were going to be worth, and ended up being foreclosed on, and having friends and family bailing them out."

"I'm a big believer in not spending before you're certain" about a wealth event, confides former M&A dealmaker Sylvia Yam. "There are no guarantees. A deal can fall apart the day before you think it will. Or, you can finish negotiating a deal, and the funds will never transfer because something will come up." Perhaps a last-minute lawsuit or a management change at the acquiring company could derail your deal.

Prior to a liquidity event, while you might be able to cash out some of your shares, most of your wealth may still exist solely on paper (and, because many things can still go astray at the 11th hour, your wealth may only hypothetically exist on paper). However, paper wealth is not the same as tangible money in the bank, and with all the uncertainties leading up to a deal in Phase 2, it's especially important not to overspend. Buying a new car should wait until after you have real cash. Besides, as many entrepreneurs already know, finding happiness while living below your means is a key to preserving your wealth and contentment.

Many of my interviewees know someone who bought a new car or a house with a liquidity event on the horizon—and was financially ruined when either the stock tanked after the IPO or a deal fell through at the last minute. Having learned from their peers' mistakes, their message is clear: don't spend before you've sold your shares, even if you think liquidity is a sure thing.

CASE STUDY
LARRY ELLISON AND THE POTENTIAL PERILS OF PREMATURE SPENDING
CO-FOUNDED ORACLE IN 1977. HIGHEST-PAID CEO IN 2008.

> The cashout-before-spending principle applies to everyone—even billionaires. The advisor to Oracle founder and chief executive Larry Ellison was nervous about how Ellison funded his spending with credit.[17] According to a 2006 *New York Times* article:
>
>> Oracle shares represent almost the entirety of Mr. Ellison's fortune, and to finance one of the country's splashiest spending sprees (454-foot megayacht, mansions, expensive hobbies, and more) he has occasionally taken on sizable

bank loans rather than sell his shares—all on the presumption that the value of his shares will remain lofty enough to allow him to pay back the loans.[18]

And that's just the tip of the iceberg: according to documents made public through a 2001 lawsuit, by 2006 Ellison had accrued $1.2 billion in loans using Oracle stock as collateral, which he used to finance his $20 million "lifestyle" spending, a $25 million Japanese villa, and a yacht budgeted for $194 million that cost $300 million—rather than sell his Oracle shares.[19]

Though Ellison's vast wealth made it unlikely these spending sprees would leave him bankrupt, his self-described "financial servant"[20] and accountant,[21] Philip Simon, convinced Ellison of the importance of caution. Selling a portion of his Oracle shares, Simon explained in an email, shouldn't be viewed as pessimistic. Rather, he asserted, "It's imperative that we start to budget and plan. New purchases should be kept to a minimum. We need to establish and execute on a diversification plan to eliminate (yes, eliminate) all debt and build up a significant, conservatively structured, liquid investment portfolio."

With genuine concern for his client, Simon acknowledged Oracle's strong balance sheet but noted, "When the pendulum swings the other way, it can overshoot. [Price-to-earnings] multiples are driven by market (or should I say, mob) psychology. There's no science or logic in the short or medium term.[22]

"I know you don't like to discuss this. I know this e-mail may/will depress you. . . . View this as a call to arms," wrote Simon. After this impassioned reality check, Ellison began paying down some of his debt.

Ellison's reluctance to sell stock in his company could have caused him much harm. In his case, the stock price remained high, and the risk he took early on by using loans—rather than cashing out Oracle shares—to fund his lifestyle paid off. After all, he was the highest paid CEO in the world in 2008 (according to Wikipedia on April 1, 2014). But what if things had been different and Oracle stock had plunged? Ellison would have been left facing $1.2 billion in debt without the equity to cover his liabilities. The banks holding the debt would likely call in their loans, and Ellison would have been forced to liquidate property.

If even a billionaire's advisor is worried about his client taking on debt without the liquidity to back it up, should you spend money you don't really have?

Bursting the Dream Bubble: Consequences of Staying in Phase 2 Longer than Expected

Not all startups reach a liquidity event, and there are plenty of entrepreneurs in their late 40s and 50s who still haven't hit the jackpot and may be wondering, "What's wrong with me?" Because the market rewards are always shifting, fortune is a huge factor in success; Lady Luck may favor the really young entrepreneurs, who can view the world with a fresh set of eyes or perhaps the older entrepreneurs, who have wisdom and experience to bring to a startup. One VC source attests to the capricious "lottery culture" of entrepreneurship, where sadly, "there are some great people who don't make money."[23]

Professor Brendan Richardson speaks from real-world experience, having worked in a variety of roles as a venture capitalist in the startup world for two decades. "Most startups don't ever get to [Phase 2]. They don't ever find the [business model] that begins to scale. And oftentimes, they pivot one or more times trying to find that scalable model. So you can bounce around in Phase 1 for many, many years, and through many, many pivots in many, many startups," Richardson admits. "I'm still in Phase 1, still chasing the dream . . . my net worth is not at a point where I don't think about work anymore."

Deal lawyer Mark Cameron White agrees that "70% of entrepreneurs in the [Silicon] Valley tried and failed, and they tried and failed again, and they tried and failed again. . . . They're living on a hope and a prayer, but they've got limited time, and I can't tell you how many companies I've worked with have great ideas, good traction, just about there, and they ran out of money. It's just a shame."

White shares a sad story about a client who spent too much on his house, lifestyle, and family, without the business success to cover his expenses. "In a society that forgives failure and actually looks at failure as being something that you want, so that people don't make the same mistake [again]," White cautions, "that can be taken to an extreme, where you ignore everything that's probably important. This guy should be getting a real job. He should not be moving to his next venture." When asked if the overspender has a financial advisor, White paused for a moment, then replied, "No, I bet you he doesn't."

If your company is stuck in Phases 1 or 2, or is swiftly running out of cash, consider a reassessment of your goals and personal assets. This is especially important if you're not independently wealthy. I suggest reviewing the Strategize section on page 109 and perhaps working with a professional financial planner to help you get a clear picture of what you've accumulated, what you spend and your future expenses (such as college education or a new home), and to create an action plan.

Checklist for Startup Founders in Phase 2

Review the items below when you are in Phase 2 to optimize your business success and personal wealth.

CORPORATE ISSUES

❑ Discuss your company's goals with your co-founders to make sure you're in agreement.

❑ Do your due diligence on executives who are introduced by your VCs. As the company ramps up toward the liquidity event, sometimes what is best for the company (and ultimately your net worth) is to replace the founder CEO with someone who has deeper business talent.

❑ Have an attorney read all contracts before you sign, to avoid last-minute fiascos or unpleasant surprises.

❑ Do your due diligence on investment bankers, including asking who or which team will work on your deal. Call references to discuss their experience with your future team.

❑ Seek out trustworthy legal advice for the company, especially if there are investment bankers involved.

PERSONAL ISSUES

❑ Prepare an inventory of your stock, options, and other equity awards. Include the vesting schedule for each award. Understanding how your equity awards work will help you maximize your wealth.

❑ If you can make an 83(b) election with little out-of-pocket cost, do so. Remember to submit an election form to both your company and the IRS, and also attach it to your tax return for the tax year in which you made the election.

❑ If you are early exercising stock options, consider hiring an accountant for personal tax and cash flow planning. If you already have assets, a financial planner with tax expertise can help you understand your cash flow and financial picture before and after your wealth event.

❑ Consult with an accountant on the personal tax impact of a sale before signing a deal to sell or merge your company. Spreading the transaction across multiple tax years or pushing income into otherwise low-income years could save significant tax dollars.

❑ Avoid spending future wealth until the deal goes through, and you have cash in hand.

❑ Hire an attorney (who may be independent of your company's attorney) to represent your personal interests before you sign contracts. Some business attorneys negotiate on behalf of their corporate clients personally.

❑ Consider hiring a coach to help you through business negotiations, management issues, or self-reflection issues, if you haven't already done so.

❑ Continue to seek out and share business advice and support from like-minded peers.

LIQUIDITY
EVENT
THE PAYOFF

The Entrepreneur's Wheel of Life[SM]

Pre-Transition Phase
2–40 years

1 Laying the Foundation

Challenges

QUALITY OF LIFE
- Preoccupation with startup
- Optimism
- Loneliness
- Improvisation
- Tenacity

FINANCIAL
- Raising capital
- Below-market salary
- Accountability to investors
- Funneling all resources into the company

Most entrepreneurs never retire.
They just keep going back to Phase 1.

Post-Transition Phase
1–24 months

3 Realizing the Dream

Challenges

QUALITY OF LIFE
- Figuring out what's next
- Determining how to return to Phase 1

FINANCIAL
- Accountability to shareholders, board, and management
- Increasing enterprise value
- Strategizing goals with financial resources
- Expensive purchases (home, car, jewelry, boat)

Pre-Transition Phase
0–24 months

2 Ramping Up

Challenges

QUALITY OF LIFE
- Maintaining balance while working long hours
- Excitement
- Persistence

FINANCIAL
- Negotiations
- Increasing enterprise value
- Compensation
- Learning new business skills
- Financial and tax planning
- Accountability to investors and board

LIQUIDITY EVENT

COMMON TO ALL PHASES

Challenge

Maximize Value of Equity Awards (ISO, NQ, RSA, RSU, ESPP)

Concerns

Wealth Preservation
Tax Reduction
Wealth Protection
Passing Assets to Heirs
Charitable Giving

Solutions

Financial Education
Expert Team of Advisors
Personal CFO

THE PAYOFF

THIS IS THE TIME YOU'VE BEEN WAITING FOR, perhaps for years or decades. You have received tangible financial proof that your idea—and the company you've created—is valuable. Outside investors want a big piece of your company.

Liquidity Event

High-tech liquidity events typically come in three flavors: a merger, an acquisition, or an IPO. Your experience in Phase 3 depends on which type of liquidity event you go through. While I won't specifically distinguish between these event types in the remainder of this book, there are some key differences I want to highlight.

MERGER OR ACQUISITION

Your company is combined with another company. It may retain its name, or not. Most likely, certain functions like HR, marketing, and legal will be merged into one operation, meaning there will be layoffs. In an acquisition, your company stock will likely be converted to shares of the acquiring company (if the deal is not done for 100% cash).

For entrepreneurs, a merger or an acquisition involves a payment in cash or stock. Be sure you fully understand the risk of accepting stock as payment. In Phase 3, the founders and executives often go to work for the new or acquiring company for a certain length of time, as may be required by the terms of the deal.

INITIAL PUBLIC OFFERING (IPO)

When the stock of your company is first offered for sale on a public stock exchange, it's known as an initial public offering. After an IPO, there's much more transparency about company activities and financials. You may be working just as hard as you did in Phase 2, because your new goal is to increase the company's stock price, as well as the value of the enterprise. New people are coming into your work family you didn't initially invite, which can be awkward.

Working at a Startup Versus a Large Company

Startup M&A attorney Michael Irvine works with people before, during, and after liquidity, helping with corporate formation and acquisition deals. In Phase 3, Irvine says, "most of them left after six months because they didn't like it. That's not what they signed on for. They had other ideas. They really liked the fact that their equity was worth a million bucks, and that was enough for them to go do something else—to take the nice vacation and then go to the next startup. If they wanted to go work for Google and have some nice RSUs that vested every 12 months, they would have gone and done that [earlier in their career]. But they didn't." Irvine often sees founders stay "for the transition, and then they're gone. Or they'll wait for that first cliff [equity vesting] and then they're gone." He generally sees nonexecutive startup employees stay for just over 12 months post-acquisition.

Another person I spoke with, who had three liquidity events, said within two years post-event the percentage of people leaving was probably over 90%. In a merger or acquisition, cultural integration issues and financial independence usually prove to be too much for these leaders to stay.[1]

If You Stay . . .

VESTING IN PEACE

Many entrepreneurs find staying on to fulfill a contractual obligation frustrating. No longer in control, they are taking orders from people who had no part creating their company. If you were the boss in Phase 2, it's entirely likely you won't be once you enter Phase 3. Some passionate startup people trudge through their contract terms, even if they only have to stay a year. "I waited a year and a day because I couldn't wait to get out of there. It was so stultifying! I was like part of the Borg," says one advisor,[2] referencing the fictional alien race that assimilates other species via violence and abduction to achieve its ultimate goal of "perfection."[3]

If you receive stock as part of a merger or acquisition deal, or you own pre-IPO shares, you may have to wait for them to vest. "VIP, vesting in peace" is how VC Lara Druyan describes this limbo time. These VIP folks just stay at the company—whether it's a new company or the same company post-IPO—and continue to vest. If there's money on the table, it's a wise wealth decision to stay and keep vesting.

INTEGRATION

Now, the company has capital, so it can continue to expand. The new people coming in don't have the upside that you once had. And it's hard for the early folks to keep up the passion they had in the early phases.

The personality traits of stubbornness, a thick skin, and incredible focus to build a successful company in Phases 1 and 2 will help you to make it through the great divide of a liquidity event. "But they're exactly the qualities you have to learn to shed," when it comes time to preserving your wealth through the vesting period of Phase 3, says Dave Buchanan, a veteran of more than a dozen high-tech companies. "You have to adapt."

Likewise, in Phase 2, "You're building excitement, you're increasing the company's valuation, in anticipation of a liquidity event," says one engineer and entrepreneur.[4] "Then you have the liquidity event which may not equal that valuation, which may not live up to all that excitement. And your 'Realizing the Dream' phase goes back to 'we need to build greater enterprise value before I can realize the dream.'"

If You Leave . . .

Though leaving means that you get to move on right away and avoid the bureaucracy that frustrates many entrepreneurs, make sure that you have a plan for your time and your money. Consult the BE WISE Planning Strategy™ (explained in a downloadable document on JLFwealth.com) for a guide to help you identify what is important to you and strategize how to make your wealth support those goals. If you plan to go back to work, like most entrepreneurs do, make sure you don't take too much time off. Technology becomes outdated quickly, and you don't want to fall behind after your well-deserved time off.

In Summary

What you'll discover after the liquidity event surprises a lot of entrepreneurs. No matter how exciting the IPO, or how many times the promise of integration is communicated, things usually are not as satisfying in Phase 3 for the true entrepreneur. Reasons may include cultural fit and new rules, or, if you're no longer working, a lack of direction. As a result, most will spend Phase 3 trying to figure out how to get back to Phase 1 of the Entrepreneur's Wheel of Life.

PHASE 3
REALIZING THE DREAM

Post-Transition Phase
1–24 Months

The Entrepreneur's Wheel of Life[SM]

Most entrepreneurs never retire.

They just keep going back to Phase 1.

1 Laying the Foundation

Pre-Transition Phase
2-40 years

Challenges

QUALITY OF LIFE
- Preoccupation with startup
- Optimism
- Loneliness
- Improvisation
- Tenacity

FINANCIAL
- Raising capital
- Below-market salary
- Accountability to investors
- Funneling all resources into the company

3 Realizing the Dream

Post-Transition Phase
1-24 months

Challenges

QUALITY OF LIFE
- Figuring out what's next
- Determining how to return to Phase 1

FINANCIAL
- Accountability to shareholders, board, and management
- Increasing enterprise value
- Strategizing goals with financial resources
- Expensive purchases (home, car, jewelry, boat)

2 Ramping Up

Pre-Transition Phase
0-24 months

Challenges

QUALITY OF LIFE
- Maintaining balance while working long hours
- Excitement
- Persistence

FINANCIAL
- Negotiations
- Increasing enterprise value
- Compensation
- Learning new business skills
- Financial and tax planning
- Accountability to investors and board

LIQUIDITY EVENT

COMMON TO ALL PHASES

Challenge
Maximize Value of Equity Awards (ISO, NQ, RSA, RSU, ESPP)

Concerns
Wealth Preservation
Tax Reduction
Wealth Protection
Passing Assets to Heirs
Charitable Giving

Solutions
Financial Education
Expert Team of Advisors
Personal CFO

PHASE 3

REALIZING THE DREAM

AFTER A LIQUIDITY EVENT, YOU ARE PROBABLY FEELING a variety of emotions from elation to satisfaction, along with some doubt. You've graduated from the intensity of Phases 1 and 2, and the next phase will likely be completely different. If you choose to stay with the company—or if you must stay because your contract requires you to—you can expect greater accountability, and therefore more pressure from the board, shareholders (if you're working for a public company), and management. Your focus may shift from innovative technology to increasing the company stock price. While you might feel some shareholder pressure at work, you may also experience some flexibility in your personal life and begin making large purchases, such as a house. If you leave the company, you may take a much-needed extended vacation.

For people who experienced financial success early in their career, this phase can be surprising, since another success is not guaranteed. This is exactly why you must make smart decisions to preserve your wealth early in Phase 3. In this chapter, you'll learn from many serial entrepreneurs who reveal how you can solidify your post-liquidity plan and allocate your newfound wealth for your future, angel investing, or other endeavors that bring the Entrepreneur's Wheel of Life full circle. As for managing your wealth, I discuss important issues unique to entrepreneurs. Do-it-yourself financial planning is explored versus the benefits of having a professional financial planner on your team.

PROFILE
THE ENTREPRENEUR'S DILEMMA: MARK GALANT

FOUNDED AND GREW GAIN CAPITAL TO BE WORTH OVER $1 BILLION IN EIGHT YEARS.

What would you do with your days if as a result of your own drive, smarts, and luck, you are so wealthy that your future great-grandchildren won't have to work?

You love the action of being an entrepreneur and building companies, but after 30 years, you want to step back from the intense 90-hour workweeks. Having achieved outsized success on their own merits, yet wanting a different lifestyle, some entrepreneurs desire change.

I was fortunate to meet Mark Galant after his liquidity event, because if I had tried to interview him while he was building his company, he would not have had the bandwidth to speak with me. In Galant's words, "As an entrepreneur, you have to work as much time as it takes to be successful, and sometimes that means you're just working all the time." While he has "made it" in every sense of the phrase, he learned some fundamental business lessons the hard way. And now that those lessons are behind him, he's carving out his ideal life. For this type-A serial entrepreneur, life and work are no longer about the money.

Forging His Own Career Path

Galant has always been entrepreneurial. After graduating from a top undergraduate business school in 1980, he broke away from the traditional career path of a 22-year-old and forged one uniquely suited to him. He knocked on doors until he found a two-person trading firm willing to place him as a Wall Street floor trader. Though his career path meandered through small companies, Harvard Business School, and then large organizations, Galant kept returning to the passion he identified early on: being a trader. This career path allowed him to take full advantage of his unique traits—his entrepreneurial spirit and the fact that he enjoys chaos, thanks to his attention deficit disorder.

As is true of most entrepreneurs, Galant was unhappy working for big companies. Fortunately, his radar was always up for opportunity. In 1999, just as retail online trading was taking off with companies like E*TRADE, he started GAIN Capital, a retail foreign currency trading business. He identified a unique niche and merged his knowledge of technology, operations, and foreign exchange trading into a sophisticated retail-trading platform. Galant willingly took a two-thirds pay cut during the first four years of business. The company received VC funding and grew rapidly. In fact, GAIN grew so quickly that in 2005 it ranked in ninth place on the Deloitte Technology Fast 500, a program that ranks North American tech companies based on percentage revenue growth over the prior four years. GAIN Capital had grown an astounding 23,318% percent during this period.[1] (For comparison: in that same year, Google came in 13th!)

Founder Liquidity

Surprisingly, during this period of gargantuan growth and high sales, in which some investors were up 70 times on their investment, Galant was butting heads with his board and VCs. He wanted to access the wealth he built inside the company, but the board resisted his requests for a liquidity event. Why? The board was afraid Galant would not be as engaged, or perhaps even leave.[2]

In Galant's experience, a company's financial success does not mean a stress-free relationship between the founder/CEO and the board. While founder cash-outs are acceptable today, thanks to the Founders Fund, back then the general rule was "never let founders and CEOs cash out . . . because they'll take their eye off the ball," says Galant. GAIN's board was focused on increasing the company's value to five times its value in just five more years. Galant kept requesting personal liquidity, and the board finally relented.

Galant soldiered on and remained at GAIN, because "running the business was fun." But after a few more years, the stress of continual disagreements with the board was taking a physical toll. VCs "think they are value-added," but Galant felt his VCs didn't have the expertise to understand his very specialized industry. He had created and grown a company of great value, worth over $1 billion in eight years (based on the 2008 valuation). Although he's a self-described type-A personality who thrives on success, the stress of dealing with the board was showing up in his body. "It's chest pain today, but this could be a heart attack months from now," realized Galant.

A Major Life Change

Just before his 50th birthday, Galant changed his life. He recalls thinking, "I'm worth a lot of money. I might as well be chairman, step back, and not have this aggravation anymore." His number two became CEO. Since the board still resisted Galant's calls for a company sale, he sold a sizable amount of his shares back to the company based on the valuation at that time. Little did he realize that this move would cost him "a tremendous amount of power," says Galant. While he knew he'd be giving up day-to-day decision making, "I was essentially equal to any other board member at that point," he remembers. "I thought at the time that I'd probably be a little more senior and have more hands in the pie. But I literally went from running the thing and being a very hands-on CEO to being there four times a year for board meetings." It took a few months for his shock to wear off.

Galant's decision to leave the company he created was bittersweet, and he's still trying to justify his internal conflict. "It is what I decided to do. And in hindsight it was a great decision. It was the right decision. The only hook was I thought I had more influence, which I didn't, but even that is OK."

After nine months off, he was bored. Hanging out by the pool every day, Galant's entrepreneurial spirit was itching to be released. He wanted to "start something again, but I didn't want it to be all-consuming." At GAIN, "I was working 90-hour weeks; if I got home at 11 at night, that would be an average day." He wanted to keep creating companies, and when he started his next venture, he took a different approach. His golden touch continues, and his current company, Tydall Trading, has achieved phenomenal success in less than three years. His take-home pay last year was more than many people accumulate in a lifetime of working. Most importantly, he's set up a corporate culture that fits his lifestyle. In his new firm, Galant has 100% ownership and a small staff, accomplishing his goal of less aggravation and more free time.

Philanthropy Begins at School

Wealth gives us choices. During Galant's nine months of downtime between the sale of most of his equity in GAIN Capital and the start of his next company, his wife encouraged him to offer his expertise in managing companies to his alma mater. Galant approached the head fundraiser at the University of Virginia, who basically turned him away with some surprising advice. "What would be better for us," said the fundraiser, since "you're good at making money, is go make more money. Donate more money, and you'll have an impact."

Thus, the Galant Center for Entrepreneurship at the University of Virginia's McIntire School of Commerce was started with a generous gift from Mark Galant. The new program consists of both undergraduate classroom work and student case competitions presented in front of potential investors. The entrepreneurship track is his contribution to encourage others. Taught by three professors with decades of experience in the startup and venture capital worlds, "Their ability to offer real-life examples and talk about their own experiences gives them instant credibility with the students and makes their teaching more effective," says Galant.[3]

Through lectures, case studies, and on-site, real-world wisdom, students are exposed to lessons others have learned the hard way. Fourth-year undergraduates take a total of four entrepreneurship courses, including two elective courses in market research, venture capital, project management, or negotiation. Focusing on teamwork, they participate in scenarios that simulate what goes on in the startup world, including generating and evaluating new business ideas, creating and presenting compelling business plans, acquiring various forms of early-stage funding, and measuring value. Importantly, the program provides a dose of reality for the students. Professor Brendan Richardson says, "Nearly every student comes in on the first day of class saying, 'I've got this great idea.' Our response is, 'That idea is literally not worth the piece of paper it's written on.'" Facing the possibility of failure is an important subject the program addresses, with the goal of becoming stronger from it.[4]

Classroom learning meets the real world at the Galant Center Challenge, a pitch competition for student startup ideas. Student groups present to venture capital and angel investors, and if the investors like what they see and hear, the presenters can receive up to $250,000 to fund their proposed business.[5] This opportunity dwarfs the much-smaller prizes of $10,000 to $25,000 awarded in similar competitions at other colleges.

It's through his ability to foster future entrepreneurs that Galant can now satisfy his passion for entrepreneurship, without the physical commitments. He hopes that entrepreneurially inclined students will commit to forming presentation groups, develop ideas during the school year, and have the opportunity to start a real company on day one after graduation.

For now, Galant is using his wealth to fund projects he is passionate about—entrepreneurship and attention deficit disorder research (also at the University of Virginia). His philosophy about philanthropy is similar to his philosophy as an entrepreneur: "When you find an idea you're passionate about, pursue it. It's been the same with our giving, so far."

Investing His Personal Fortune

For his personal investing, Galant uses exchange traded funds (ETFs). The advantage for him is that they keep his tax liability very low. In his trading business, Galant trades thousands of times a day, in millionths of a second. Yet, this Wall Street veteran prefers a buy-and-hold ETF allocation for his personal portfolio. Even more telling, he says that when he trades his own money in ETFs, he's achieved better performance than the Wall Street advisors he hires.

After a Big Success, Now What?

But conflict is again percolating inside Galant's always-active mind. It's possible that never being satisfied unless your business is growing rapidly at its optimum capacity is inherent to entrepreneurs, both fueling and guiding their success. The ability to completely dedicate your time and mental energy to the task at hand, and the inability to take no for an answer, often leads to success in business. Because of Tydall's tremendous growth, Galant could scale it and be even more financially successful—if it weren't for the resource commitment.

"I should probably have at least twice the amount of employees that I have, and I just don't want to. I'm worried about intellectual property leaking and people leaving and the aggravation of managing more people. I'm keeping the number of people I have employed much lower than it probably should be."

Now in his mid-50s, Galant has sculpted his idea of a great life: working less than 20 hours a week in the office, although he constantly monitors email and analyzes currency charts in his round-the-clock trading business; traveling; golfing; and spending time with his wife and adult children. And at this point, earning more would not affect his lifestyle one bit.

Yet, there is a part of Galant that misses the thrill of growing his own company. To satisfy this desire, he's started dabbling in angel investing, which enables him to mentor and grow young companies without taking on day-to-day responsibilities.

"I like to try to relax when I get a chance," says Galant from his hot tub, where, he informs me, he has been sitting during our entire 90-minute phone interview.

Galant's Lessons Learned

- Negotiate up front (in the early stages of your startup) for the ability to take cash out if the company is doing well. Terms of a cash-out deal could occur either from selling your shares to investors or going public. While a rising company valuation is terrific, it's frustrating when you can't access your wealth.

- Entrepreneurs have to be very flexible to be successful. "In general you have to plan and sketch [the business plan] out." However, "putting it in writing and getting too focused on it is not necessarily good, because you have to improvise so much as an entrepreneur." It's best to have "broad brush goals" that you want to achieve.

- If the majority of your net worth is tied up in your company, it's easy to be too cautious. "Take more risks," says Galant. "In my case, spend more on marketing."

- On hiring: "As an employer—an entrepreneurial employer—I'd rather see someone who's tried and failed, and I'd rather hire him than someone who came from a big [company]."

- On funding: "Use as little of your own money as possible because [startups are] very risky. It's very easy to do a startup, and there could be three other competitors that have already done it or are months ahead of you, or years ahead of you."

- On VCs: "If you're a 25-year-old kid who has never run a company before, they probably can add a lot of value. But, if you're 40 years old and have run a lot of stuff, they can be more of a hindrance sometimes."

- "Be careful what you wish for, because you might not get the control that you want," if you step down as the CEO, says Galant. As a founder who is no longer running the company, you will likely lose control of it. "If you give up the CEO reins . . . whatever you have still left in the company is under someone else's discretion. It's not yours anymore."

Concentrated Stock Positions

The opposite of concentration, diversification spreads your investments between many companies across the globe, so you avoid putting all of your eggs in one basket.

Mark Galant recognized the need to diversify out of his company stock. However, many entrepreneurs aren't so proactive about diversification. After a liquidity event, people often become greedy or naïve about diversifying a concentrated stock position in their own company. Subsequently, company stock can grow to a larger and larger share of your net worth. An entrepreneur and former executive at a networking equipment company prefers to describe this brand of enthusiasm as "belief"—but what gets people into trouble is the misguided "belief that things only go up, and not being realistic about how quickly they can come down again."[6]

Serial entrepreneur Marc Tarpenning explains that this reluctance may be because "the engineering community tries to be analytical but has a real emotional attachment to their particular [company] stock." His own rationale for diversifying? "Maybe it's going to get higher, maybe it's going to get lower, but you should get something out of it, whether it's to put a down payment on the house, or buy a new car. . . . You worked on this, and you put your heart and soul into it. . . . The worst thing to do is run out of money, because then it forces you to make non-optimal decisions." See the Decision Tree analysis on page 117 to help you determine a way out of a concentrated position that works for you.

Although it's impossible to determine the right time to sell, issues arise when you're "anchoring" on a historical stock price that may never be reached again. It's important to strike a balance between holding on to all of your stock out of belief in your company, and avoiding selling out too early. One thing is for sure: daily monitoring the stock price in search of that balance pulls you and your team away from your job. A strategy that works for some is to set price targets on the stock so that it will be sold automatically when a certain price is reached.

It's tough to emotionally distance yourself from the stock price of the company you have built. Plus, selling shares only to see the company stock price rise faster than a diversified portfolio makes some post-IPOers wonder, "Why did I work so hard and now not continue to recognize these upsides?"[7]

Some founders and executives believe selling company stock is a signal they no longer believe in their company, yet protecting the assets you worked so hard to amass means getting out of a concentrated position. Selling stock to protect your wealth from unforeseen corporate slings and arrows should not be viewed as an indication of your faith in the company.

HOW A BILLIONAIRE DIVERSIFIES

Even billionaire high-tech veteran Eric Schmidt diversifies. After reigning as Google's CEO for 10 years, he stepped down in April 2011 and now serves as executive chairman, still committed to the company. The *Wall Street Journal* reports Schmidt filed to sell 40% of his Google stock, or 3.2 million shares, in 2013 and early 2014, and as of the time of this writing,[8] those 3.2 million shares are valued at $2.5 billion. After the sale, his personal exposure to the stock of Google will decrease by more than half over two years. In a statement from the company, Schmidt's plan was described "as part of his long-term strategy for individual asset diversification and liquidity,"[9] and is worthy of taking note.

Sell Some, as Soon as You Can: Martin Eberhard

Many of my interviewees talked about a strategy in which they sold half of the stock as soon as they could. "My advice to anybody involved in a startup company," offers Tesla Motors founder Martin Eberhard, "is the minute you have liquidity, sell half. It's not a vote of confidence against the company to diversify. If you don't, and the stock goes down—and I've watched many, many of my friends let it ride down to zero—you're going to feel terrible. And if it goes up, you still have that other half to ride up, but you also have your nest egg." Eberhard is not as stringent with the other half. "Once I've sold half, I've taken a lot more than I put into the company." For that Eberhard is very fortunate, since such consistent success doesn't happen as often as you might think.

To the extent he can do so, Eberhard formulates his own plan for selling his company stock. When his pre-Kindle ebook company, NuvoMedia, was acquired, he was unable to sell for six months due to his executive position. Then, the company kept him from selling shares by delaying its S-3 filing. "And so I hammered them and hammered them to get the S-3 done." He and his co-founder continued to lean on the company, resorting to legal pressure to get the filing completed. "And because I had such a bad feeling about that company, I sold all of [my stock] immediately, every single share, at the first opportunity." Eberhard's strategy paid off: While he lost about 20% of the stock's value by the time he could sell, he saw a vice president ride the stock down from approximately $110 to $3 per share.

Eberhard showed the same tenacity when he sold his Tesla stock: "In fact, the day that we could sell was my wife's birthday, and we were in Maui. I was up at two in the morning selling stock as fast as I could. I sold about 90% of what I held in the first 20 minutes of trading."

In addition to diversifying, the other key to Eberhard's financial success is that he outsources what he cannot or does not want to do.

> "I'm an engineer. I want to think about engineering;
> money is boring."
> —Martin Eberhard, founder of Tesla Motors

Eberhard wisely understands the dangers of do-it-yourself investing and taxes. After the IPO of his first company, he recognized that he wasn't going to track his personal finances every day and he realized it was time to hire someone who would: "I did my own taxes with TurboTax up until NCD's [Network Computing Devices] IPO. Then, it was too hard. I could have done it, but it would have consumed me. Unless you're on top of the money every single day, you need to pay for somebody who is, or you're going to lose it. My portfolio is so diverse right now, and [my advisor is] constantly looking at it."

Outsourcing works for him, because he has a strong rapport with his advisor: "I put huge amounts of trust in my financial advisor, and it has taken me decades to build that trust. If she advises me to do something, I generally take her advice." His advisor also has a level of expertise that Eberhard doesn't. "It's really hard to diversify enough that you're actually diverse—not correlated— and you can't do that on your own. It's really complex, and unless you're on top of it, you're throwing your money away."

"I don't really like playing with money very much," Eberhard explains. "But on the other hand I do care about getting wiped out financially. A lot." His motivation for hiring an advisor is to preserve his wealth, so he can continue to create great companies, exercise his creative muscle, and retain his financial freedom.

Even my husband, a tech entrepreneur, didn't understand the impact of smart planning until after his liquidity event. Then, he was thrilled at the tax mitigation and wealth preservation guidance I—acting as his personal financial planner—provided.

My Husband's Liquidity Event & Our Wise Planning Strategy

My husband sold his company in 2008. I'd been helping clients through sudden-money events for nearly 15 years, but it wasn't until his company's sale that I learned the emotional side of a liquidity event firsthand—including the excitement, negotiation, realization it might not happen, and finally the completion of the deal.

While the deal with Autodesk, a large 3D design, engineering, and entertainment software company,[10] was all cash and my husband's net worth was not tied to the new company's stock price, he did have a contractual obligation to remain at the acquiring company. Thus, Autodesk's financial statements—which he did not control and hardly could influence—were now important to our family's future. Additionally, I learned the emotional impact that a dip in the stock market can have after a recent, very large investment. Applying emotional detachment to the investment meant that the long-term value of our portfolio was secured. This was a great opportunity for me to put into practice several smart financial planning moves that had a big impact on my family's future.

In January 2008, we invested the first and largest tranche of my husband's (after-tax) sales proceeds in the stock market. We considered dollar cost averaging, but decided against it for two reasons: he would receive two more payout tranches, and our investment time horizon was very long-term. Since we were relatively young and it would be at least 15 or 20 years before we would need the cash, we could weather a market downturn of our nest egg.

Fate then took an interesting turn. Beginning that summer, the broad stock market started to plunge: it was the beginning of the Great Recession, and the market was melting. Between the summer of 2008 and the bear market low on March 9, 2009, I reviewed our investment portfolio often to "harvest" and realize the losses we had from the market's drop. Selling one position and buying a similar but not identical holding to retain market exposure is what I do anyway for my clients during market downturns.

In those 15 months between when we invested my husband's proceeds from a decade of hard work and the low point in the bear market, I had successfully preserved—or realized—losses of an amount equal to approximately 30% of the cash he invested in January 2008. We essentially used these losses to offset the gain from the sale of his company. This is a big deal, so I'll say it again: my execution of our investment management strategy reduced the taxes on the sale of my husband's company by 30% because of tax loss harvesting.

As of this writing, six years after his exit, returns from the broad stock market (using the Russell 3000 Index as a benchmark) have recovered from the 2008 plunge.[11] While the stock market has returned to its pre-bear-market level, my husband locked in his losses at the low point, successfully using them to offset the gain from the sale of his company. Not only did he pay less tax on the sale of his company, but the clincher here is that his portfolio retained exposure to the stock market throughout the turbulence. Over the six-year market cycle, he maintained his principal and the exposure to the stock market we need to meet our long-term goals.

The stock market is a volatile place, and you can be sure to experience many years in which your portfolio returns a loss. While we hope we will never again experience a bear market like the Great Recession, any time you see unrealized losses in a taxable account, selling the position and "harvesting" the loss while retaining your asset allocation is a valuable tax-mitigation strategy for everyone.

Before he met me, my husband considered most advisors to be the unskilled equivalent of "vacuum cleaner salespeople" and didn't understand the benefit an advisor could add. Based upon our experience in the down market, he realized the value of having a professional advisor.

People are often irrational with their own money, which is why a thoughtful, unemotional financial planner is necessary. Turning a market downturn into a tax-minimizing event, and staying focused on long-term goals rather than the current value of your portfolio, can make you wealthier in the long term.

When I was planning for my family, I found it useful to break down the process into steps I call the BE WISE Planning Strategy. This is a process I use with clients, too.

The BE WISE Planning Strategy: A Formula for Financial Success & Personal Happiness

To have a satisfying life, it's important to identify your passions and your goals.

I call the process of discovering and planning for life before, during, and after an IPO or other wealth event **BE WISE: Before Event, Work, Identify, Strategize, Execute.**

Before Event
Create a business plan incorporating your goals for your company and your career, which will likely include some of your personal values.

Work
Build your company. Consult with a CPA or comprehensive financial planner about tax planning with your equity awards. Entrepreneurs: Strategize the ideal corporate and equity award structure, and hire an attorney to create contracts, early exercise elections, and vesting schedules.

Identify
Identify what's important to you. How will you spend your time if your company is sold, acquired, or goes public? Don't be caught without a plan.

Strategize
Determine if your assets will support your goals and values. Carve out a "Maintain Bucket" for long-term lifestyle needs. Allocate excess capital into "Risk," "Give," and other buckets, if needed.

Execute
Implement and monitor specific action items as a road map to achieve your goals, preserve your wealth, minimize risk and taxes, and pass along assets to those you care about.

While the last two stages are chronological—your plan is analyzed, then action steps are created and executed, with or without the assistance of a financial planner—Work and Identify should happen together. For a more detailed description of the BE WISE Planning Strategy, a guide to help you plan for your personal and financial future, and a profile of a well-known entrepreneur who used it successfully, download the white paper available at JLFwealth.com.

STRATEGIZE: MAINTAIN, RISK & GIVE

Life is expensive. If you know where you want to go, a financial plan can help you highlight any gaps that may exist along the way. Strategizing your goals and how to use your assets should occur directly after a liquidity event. The timing is important, because if too much time goes by post-liquidity, you may lose out on planning and wealth creation opportunities. Here you will determine, through quantitative analysis, if your assets will support your goals, values, and interests for the remainder of your life. If you have excess, you get to decide what to do with this pot of funds—the cherry on top.

First, list your goals. Here are some examples of short-term financial goals:

- Purchase a $2 million home in San Francisco within the next 12 months.
- Travel to Asia next year for two months, spending $30,000.
- Protect your dependents and yourself with insurance coverage, allowing your family to continue in its existing lifestyle if an unexpected accident or illness occurs.

Some long-term financial objectives may include:

- Fund your children's four-year private university education beginning in 10 years.
- Accumulate (or preserve) funds to maintain your current lifestyle during retirement.
- Provide for your dependents and heirs.

The second step is to assess your resources and evaluate your ability to reach both your personal and financial goals. Unrealistic goals lead to frustration, and planning now to avoid disappointment later is a major component of the

Strategize phase of the BE WISE Planning Strategy. Recognize that your goals will shift over time. Therefore, you should review them whenever life-changing events occur. At my firm, we recommend that our clients review their goals annually, at a minimum.

To protect your finances and reach these goals, divide your wealth into categories, specifically a "Maintain Bucket," a "Risk Bucket," and a "Give Bucket."

❶ The Maintain Bucket. The first bucket should consist of what you need to comfortably live out your life. This money is what you need to maintain your lifestyle; extensive analytical work, often under the guidance of a financial planner, should be done to determine this amount. Never dip into this pile for extra angel investment capital or other risky ventures. It's crucial to make sure the assets in your Maintain portfolio are invested in a prudent, risk-appropriate way.

❷ The Risk Bucket. The second pot contains exploration funds; you can use this money for angel investing, self-managed investments, starting a new company—whatever you like. This second pot should never be merged with the first. Make sure you have enough money to support your lifestyle, even if all of your Risk portfolio investments fail.

❸ The Give Bucket. If you are charitably inclined, the third pot is for making donations to your favorite causes.

CARVING OUT WHAT YOU CAN RISK

"Everything in the Valley is high risk," says transactional attorney Mark Cameron White, so the personal challenge is coming up with a portfolio of your net worth that delineates risk and non-risk capital. One of his entrepreneur clients, for example, made hundreds of millions, and now forgoes risky new ventures for very conservative diversified investments; another client risks some, but not much. Both founders have carved out (at least) what they need for the rest of their lives, and only take chances with the money in their Risk Bucket, knowing their lifestyles will be protected.

Before you divide your assets into the Maintain, Risk, and Give Buckets (or more), you'll want to understand what you have, how long it will last, and how to protect it. The best way to gain a thorough understanding is to perform an analysis, preferably with an experienced and knowledgeable advisor or a qualified family member, friend, or co-worker. However, be wary of any tax implications. If you work with a financial planner, he or she should prepare the following documents and analyses:

❶ **Net Worth Statement.** This document should include an inventory of your assets and liabilities. Life insurance should be accounted for here, as well. Identify whether you have adequate property and casualty insurance to protect your assets from unintended loss (from natural disasters, theft, or inattention) or from being unjustly taken in a lawsuit.

❷ **Cash Flow Projection.** Determines inflows and outflows of cash on an after-tax basis, to show yearly surpluses or deficits. An ongoing (or large one-time) cash surplus may allow for increased spending, the ability to take on less risk in the portfolio, or earlier financial independence. A deficit requires strategizing on how best to fund your needs and how to provide a sustainable cash flow in a tax-efficient way.

❸ **Financial Independence Projection.** An analysis shows if your assets can help you achieve your goals. Tweaking your plan may be warranted here. For example, if you want to use cash savings to invest in new companies, it's important to know how much you could afford to lose and still achieve your most important goals. This step determines how much goes to your Maintain Bucket, and how much you have left to risk or give.

❹ **Insurance Analyses.** Calculate how best to protect your and your family's lifestyle in the event of an illness, disability, or other catastrophe.

Strategizing a plan and carving out a Maintain Bucket after your liquidity event, however, means very little if you fail to execute it. You need to act quickly with these decisions, because the market won't wait for you. Joe Preis (profiled in the sidebar) is a perfect example of how just one planning tactic can mean the difference between earning a fortune and holding worthless stock.

PROTECTING WEALTH VIA A CASHLESS COLLAR: JOE PREIS

SOLD METRORENT TO CENDANT FOR CASH AND STOCK IN 1999. SOLD
MOVE.COM DOMAIN TO CENDANT IN A SEPARATE ALL-CASH DEAL.

In the early 1990s, Joe Preis purchased a small San Francisco apartment-finding service, MetroRent, and grew it to a successful target for his liquidity event.[12] With a Stanford MBA and a lifelong interest in real estate, he figured he could make some tweaks to the business operations and create a nice cash cow business for himself. Though Preis immediately implemented strategic changes—such as opening the office on nights and weekends, so it would be more accessible to apartment hunters in the pre-Internet days—MetroRent sales didn't explode until the mid-'90s when the Internet took off and Preis put apartment listings online. His forte had always been to combine real estate and technology, and he was in his element.

Speaking with fellow travelers on a 1998 trip to Israel helped Preis realize what a gem he owned. When the inevitable "What do you do?" question arose, Preis was surprised to find that most people not only recognized MetroRent, but actually used it. Since his company was well known and Preis identified as financially conservative, he decided to find a buyer and cash out.

After a year spent hunting with his investment banker, he signed a deal with a competitor who lacked strength in the privately owned apartment rental market. The deal was 55% cash (3/5 up front and 2/5 paid as an earnout over three years) and 45% phantom stock in a company that had not yet gone public. The earnout was based on performance goals, and to his surprise the corporate office did not help him meet the benchmarks. As it became clear he was no longer in control of his own financial success—he was now running a tiny operation in a very large corporation—he became frustrated and concerned about his earnout cash and the value of his stock.

Through activity of his parent company in 1999, his phantom stock was converted into newly public shares of Homestore. Preis wanted to take action to protect his net worth—a large portion of which was held in Homestore stock—because he was nervous about the company's future. But still in the lockup period from the deal, he couldn't sell his shares outright for another year. Preis discussed his growing unease with a colleague from his entrepreneurs' group, who suggested he use a cashless collar (see page 162 for a description of what a collar is and how to use one). He soon collared his stock at $33 per share (the fair market value that day) with a downside limit of $30 and an upside of $39. One year later, when he was contractually able to sell his stock and diversify, the stock price was $0.33 per share, dramatically lowered both by the 2000 dot-com wreckage and fraud at the parent company. Preis sold his shares at $30 per share, the downside limit on his cashless collar. The protection his colleague suggested made a huge difference in his total payout.

After taking a several-year break from work—too long, he admits, as "more than one year off is dangerous," because that's long enough to fall behind on technology—he has started a business combining his passions for technology, finance, and real estate in the residential market.

How Much Is Enough?

For most people, the dollar amount of "enough" shifts upwards as your wealth grows. Modest IPO wealth can make life easier by taking a lot of financial pressure off. But at the same time, young people are looking ahead at a long road to retirement, plus a lot of big cash outlays[13] for such things as their children's education. This means your wealth must last a long time.

When asked if she understood the risk consequences of holding equity awards such as restricted stock and options, an ex-Googler replied thoughtfully, "There's a difference between rationally understanding it, and emotionally understanding it." If the stock price goes down, that's real wealth lost; but emotionally, it's harder to contemplate the downside and diversify out of the rising stock of your own company.[14]

In order to counteract the stock market's pull on your emotions, it's best to be disciplined when you hold stock options and company stock. One senior engineer, who watched the stock of the hot tech company he worked for crash during the dot-com downturn, contends, "People believe that because the stock was once at $80, it will get back there. It may never get back there."[15]

Why Do People Hold?

Once the lockup period ends—and in certain cases, even earlier—those involved in a startup can sell their company stock and escape from a concentrated position. But I've heard and seen in practice that most don't make this logical move. Some people never get around to selling, and they continue to hold on to their hard-won reward even as the stock value shrivels up.

To find out why, I asked interviewees: What paralyzes people, fear of missing an opportunity or not knowing about alternate investments, or greed from the prospect of the stock price increasing? Responses were an even and overwhelming split between greed alone, and a combination of both fear and greed.

Fear and Greed

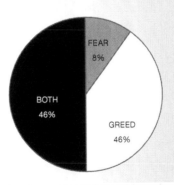

Figure 4. The chart above factors in responses from 35 interviewees.

Many people refused to even talk in these terms. Fear and greed, they argued, had too many negative connotations. Instead, they said that fear was "worry" about the alternative use of the sales proceeds, and greed was "optimism" or "enthusiasm" for the company they helped to build. Those who could not decide between the two often replied "both," because worrying about losing out on future appreciation had the same importance to them as enthusiasm for the company.

Some interviewees[16] simply couldn't identify the emotions involved, and others avoided the question entirely. The passionate reaction to the terms used, the confusion over the motivation for holding, and the difficulty in answering a seemingly simple either/or question all indicate that the issue is both complicated and emotionally charged. Whatever the true reason that people hold on to their company stock, it's clear that investment decisions invoke intense emotional reactions, and not everyone can separate "gut feeling" from the grounded, rational choices that must be made for successful investing.

PEOPLE ARE MORE RATIONAL WITH STOCK TODAY

"There's not a lot of holding," today, says venture capital and high-tech business attorney Jim Koshland. "The problem with the dot-com heyday is most [employees] had lockups, and the trading window before the market meltdown did not leave much time for selling." When the crash came in early 2001, the stock price for many companies went down so fast, employees didn't have time to cash out.[17] The solution to blackout periods for executives is a 10b5-1 plan (see tip on page 161).

When friends or clients ask VC Sonja Hoel Perkins how much stock they should hold in their companies, she deftly turns the question back to them: "Would you buy that stock today?"

How to Sell Stock During Blackout Periods: Use a 10b5-1 Plan

For entrepreneurs, selling company stock can be tricky, as the stock transactions of executives and board members of public companies are visible to the public via SEC filings. One entrepreneur/executive I spoke with who served on the boards of two Fortune 500 companies received stock as compensation for being a director and cautions that selling stock should be done "in a smart, ethical way. If you're a CEO or an officer of a company, you just can't diversify"[18] without understanding and legally complying with the rules of insider trading. However, a 10b5-1 plan, which is relatively new, allows selling based on a predetermined schedule or trigger point, and will keep you in compliance of the law while minimizing risk of concentration in the stock of your company.

A 10b5-1 plan exists to solve the problem of concentrated positions by legally ignoring blackout windows. Read more about this strategy in the Tips section at the end of this chapter.

"I tend to sell over time now," says Yahoo CFO Ken Goldman, a 30-year high-tech veteran.[19] "I use a 10b5 over time, because I don't have the ability to game it. It's just easier as a CFO to use a 10b5 than try to figure out open windows. I think there's a certain group of people that want to hold on and ride it out because they believe so strongly. Financial advisors would tell you to take some money off the table, just average it out, and manage it over time, which I tend to agree with."

Averaging the sales out over time, in a methodical way, gives you a higher chance of capturing the wealth you've created. "You're always ticked off when you think you sell too early, you're ticked off if you think you sell too late," rationalizes Goldman. "There's always seller's remorse."

When asked about the experiences that allow people to hold on to their net worth after an IPO, Goldman offers the following advice:

- "If you already have plenty—more than you ever thought you needed or will need—then it's easier to play it for the long term.

- "If you have pressing debts to repay, or commitments to certain things you want to buy right away, you tend to get forced to sell some earlier.

- "If you're in a position where you're totally well-off, then the only question is when to take some off the table, so you don't look stupid in case the stock does go down. But on the other hand, you can ride it [if you] believe the company will do very well, and you'll participate in that. And if it doesn't work perfectly, at least you still feel confident you already have enough net worth that [your personal balance sheet] is not going to be negative."

Another high-tech executive who has been involved in multiple high-profile acquisitions says this about the time before 10b5-1 plans became available: "In one of the companies, I was constantly locked up because I always knew that material events were occurring and was unable to sell my shares. [Other] people made millions and millions during that time. If I could have, I would have diversified."[20] Her advice to anyone working at a publicly traded company is to "have a 10b5 plan in place so that as soon as you get the shares, you sell them. Don't hold them." An auto-sell strategy means, "you're really maximizing your value."

A 10b5-1 plan is great for the company, too. One employee of a hot tech company who didn't have a 10b5-1 plan told me that during the first six months after the IPO, she checked the stock price—hourly—to figure out the best time to sell. That came at the company's expense. When she was checking the stock price, she wasn't focused on her work. I heard this story over and over from sources involved in IPOs.

A Rule 10b5-1 plan is generally set up by a law firm or your company using a template. The plan is a contract between the broker, the company, and the employee. To avoid any appearance of insider trading, it's best not to make modifications, terminations, or suspensions to a plan. Therefore, set up your personal plan only after thoughtful consideration of your individual situation during the plan's time horizon—likely for years, or until you leave the company.

THE OPTIMISM TRAP

Entrepreneurs are inherently optimistic people; in fact, it's their inveterate optimism that contributes to their success. But when it comes to investing their windfall, it can get them into trouble. The optimism bias is a well-known behavioral finance quirk. When confronted with a fat-tail set of outcomes, the optimist thinks disproportionately about the fat-tail on the right: "I can become a billionaire if I just hold on!" Little attention is paid to the fat tail on the left: "I can go broke in several different ways." Thus, the very quality of optimism that contributes to entrepreneurs' success may be torpedoing their subsequent preservation of their fortune.[21]

Decision Tree Analysis: A Rational Approach to a Concentrated Equity Position

How do you overcome your emotions about your company stock and decide if—and how much—to diversify? A Decision Tree Analysis can provide a quantitative—and rational—perspective on when and how much stock to sell.

It is often incredibly difficult to make rational decisions concerning your newly acquired wealth. If you are an analytical type and hold in-the-money options or a concentrated stock position, then a decision tree using probability analysis is a valuable way to assess your best course of action. This tool is much more helpful than basing your sell or hold decision on gut feeling.

Individuals and companies use decision trees to help understand how to evaluate risk and ambiguity. People often make non-optimal decisions when they adopt a skewed perception of their choices. In the case of a concentrated equity position, overconfidence and the enthusiasm that accompanies a recent success can cloud decisions. The decision tree combats this uncertainty by providing a clear and logical set of outcomes for a participant to choose from, based

Sample Decision Tree

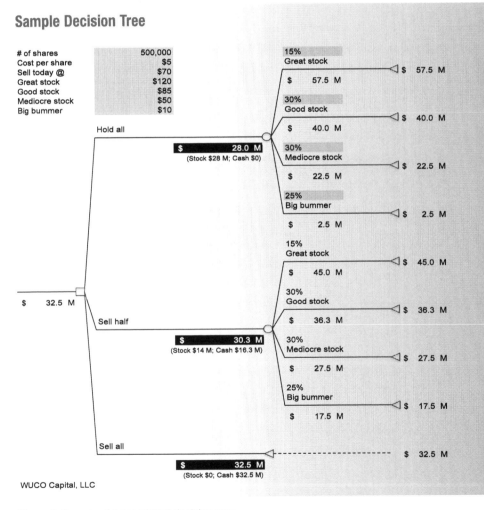

Figure 5. Sample of a completed decision tree.

ingeniously on probabilities assigned by the participant. Assigning probabilities to each outcome and following the logical progression of each decision point can be an eye-opening exercise, especially for an analytical engineer.

THE DECISION TREE: HOW IT WORKS

This decision tree format comes originally from the Stanford Decision Analysis graduate program. The sample decision tree on page 118 was created by engineer, entrepreneur, CEO, and investor Peter Herz to be used by someone holding a concentrated equity position.[22] Let's call the equity holder in this example "John." John holds a concentrated position in stock options, founders' stock, or pre-IPO shares. To create the tree, John would first populate all values in the top left corner of the graphic that have a light gray background: the number of shares he owns (500,000), his cost per share ($5), and the current trading price of the stock ($70). Second, he assigns a dollar-value threshold for how much the stock must be worth in order for him to consider it a "great stock," "good stock," "mediocre stock," or "big bummer."

John then determines the subjective values, namely the future stock price and the relative percentage likelihood of the stock reaching the specific outcomes. The analytically minded Herz explains the tree matter-of-factly: "The way decision trees work is the square is a decision point, the circles are events with probabilistic outcomes paths, and the triangles are endpoints. If you sell everything, you go straight to an endpoint. If you either sell half or hold all, you're then at a place where there will be a probabilistic outcome depending on what happens to the stock. And the way I set it up, I actually make the probability of the big bummer whatever's left after you divide up the odds for the great stock, the good stock, and the mediocre stock outcomes. And that helps, because then [the participant holding the concentrated position] doesn't have to think about the big bummer, and it just ends up being whatever it is." The three dollar values in the middle column are the probability-weighted outcomes of each path, ranging from $32.5 million of cash in the "sell all" scenario to $28 million of stock in the "hold all" scenario.

Herz believes it's really important that the person who has the shares and decisions to make is the person who assigns the probabilities. "If you change the [probabilities or future stock price values], it could be that one of these other paths ends up being the best path, and that number inherits whatever the best of these three paths are."

The focus of the decision tree is to avoid the chance of the worst possible outcome. "No matter how unlikely you think that probability is, you don't want to be on that [branch] of the decision tree" that will produce a catastrophic outcome. He points to the "hold all" branch explaining, "If you don't pick this path of the tree, you will never get there," pointing to the "big bummer" result of $2.5 million (a bad result in this case, only because of what the other, better choices could have returned). Herz then acknowledges this strategy also eliminates the best outcome, in which John holds everything and the stock price shoots up. "By designing out [the part of the tree with the worst result], you are leaving [a potentially] huge outcome on the table, but you're also eliminating the crap-tastic outcome of losing almost everything."

Herz applies an unemotional broad-brushstroke view to his personal startup equity. "I, as a rule, sell half, and that way I'm always half-right, and also half-wrong." His takeaway message: If you're not on "the branch that says you're holding everything, you can never get to the lose everything [result]."

THE DECISION TREE MECHANICS
The probabilities in each branch must total 100%, because there is a 100% certainty that the stock price will exist in one of these ranges. However, the price could be higher than the great stock price or lower than the big bummer price. But since the future is unknown, John is guessing when he assigns the probabilities to his tree. For example, at a stock price of $70, John thinks there is a 15% chance of the stock being great and reaching $120 per share, a 30% chance of it being good and reaching $85 per share, a 30% chance of it being mediocre and dropping to $50 per share, and a 25% chance of it being a "big bummer" and plummeting to $10 per share.

The values to the right of the triangles represent John's potential sale outcomes, which range from $2.5 million to $57.5 million. Because the first branch holds the highest outcome, it's tempting to immediately gravitate toward the "hold all" option. However, take a look at the two bottom black rectangles of the middle column. These are the "expected values" of each branch, or simply the sum of all the smaller branches to the right of the circles (sale price less cost per share, multiplied by the assigned probability in that branch), the average return John can expect to make. In the "hold all" branch, the expected value is calculated as follows:

$$\text{Expected Value} = \$28,000,000$$
$$= (\$57,500,000 \times .15) + (\$40,000,000 \times .30) +$$
$$(\$22,500,000 \times .30) + (\$2,500,000 \times .25)$$

Given the information John knows today, by holding all of his stock he can expect it will be worth $28 million. Yet two of the "hold all" branches would give him a worse result than this, and the stock price could drop (or increase) at any moment. Herz further explains that $28 million "should then be compared to the expected value of the other branches. The optimal value is the number that's ultimately shown all the way to the left [$32.5 million]; the path that produces [$32.5 million] is the path or paths that have that value in the middle column." It is the "sell all" scenario in this example that leads to the highest expected value.

Depending on the assigned probabilities, John could end up with a better outcome on the "sell half" or "hold all" branches of the tree. "For example," says Herz, if John decides "the great stock outcome has a 35% probability and [the] big bummer only a 5% probability, then 'hold all' becomes the best economic choice." Of course, the value of held shares can change at any moment.

APPLYING THE DECISION TREE TO YOUR CONCENTRATED STOCK OR OPTION POSITION

The decision tree is a valuable tool to use in conjunction with the BE WISE Planning Strategy for identifying your goals and strategizing how best to deploy assets (see page 108). If you're holding a concentrated position, this rational approach to assessing the probability of each outcome is an eye-opening way to determine the best course of action. It's a dramatically easy means of giving you valuable perspective on your choices.

A SERIAL ENTREPRENEUR'S VIEW OF PHASE 3
BALANCING FEAR AND GREED WITH A TARGET PRICE STRATEGY.

Many entrepreneurs I spoke with do not enjoy Phase 3, and generally live in it just as long as they need to for vesting or transition purposes while concurrently in Phase 1 of another venture. Like most founders I spoke with for this book, one source said he does not expect to ever be part of "a Fortune 50 company. That would be painful for me."[23]

Fear, Greed & Selling in Phase 3

Having been involved as a founder, executive, or investor in many deals in the last 25 years, this source believes that "people don't have a very good balance of fear and greed." His advice: "When fear overcomes greed, sell. Or when greed overcomes fear, sell. One or the other.

"I think it's really, really hard for people to be content, because we're still living in a society where people always want more," says the engineer and entrepreneur. "If your stock is going up five points a week, then you say, 'I'll wait two weeks. I'll sell at 10 points more.' But they don't think about what if it's down 10 points tomorrow. It's just a very difficult thing for people to do. I think that greed is powerful and Gordon Gekko was right," he says, referencing Michael Douglas's indelible character in the 1987 movie *Wall Street*. But, this source says, "You need to counterbalance that."

Most founders agree that a liquidity event is not an end, but just a beginning. There are more people to answer to, and the company must continue to grow. The engineer and entrepreneur advises that "just because you got acquired doesn't necessarily mean that you're off the hook" in terms of performance: "In most cases when you get acquired, you're on the hook for at least a year. If you IPO, you're on the hook for at least six months, until you can become liquid. And if you're an officer of the company, you're dealing with 10b5-1 programs and all sorts of stuff to actually get liquid. So there isn't this immediate gratification day. It's more of a next step on the way."

Personal Finances and Diversification

Ever since he took his first company public in the dot-com heyday, this engineer and entrepreneur has followed the same strategy to determine when to sell stock. And he advises others to follow his lead.

Before the IPO, he writes down a number. It's his best guess at a valuation he'd be happy selling at, and when the stock price hits that value, he sells everything he can. Since he is usually not fully vested when the stock reaches his sell target, he'll sell all vested shares at his preset target value. Generally, he'll be able to sell at least half of his shares. He waits to sell the remainder of his shares as they vest in the future, in what he calls a "sell ladder," expecting to average out at a certain price.

He doesn't use his own money to finance his own ventures: "I am a firm believer in leveraging other people's money as much as possible. But I'm willing to give up ownership for it to be fair."

Outsourcing Finances to Professionals

Over more than two decades, this source has earned various types of equity awards, including ISOs and non-qualified stock options. He outsources the management of his finances to trusted advisors to track the vesting of his shares and to understand how holding periods and option types affect his taxes. "When a large portion of my tax bill became influenced on my option and stock selling strategy, that's when I knew it was time to get help," he remembers. "You can solve a lot of problems with time and money. And I just didn't have time, so I solved it with money. It's always a time versus money equation. And if I can spend money to buy time, I will."

Armed with his target stock price strategy and loyal colleagues from various startups and board positions, he has smartly accumulated wealth and achieved prominence in his field. He continues to be pleased with his decision to outsource both tax and financial management to professionals he likes and trusts.

Hire a Professional Advisor or Do It Yourself?

After a liquidity event, you have an important decision to make. Will you manage your finances yourself or outsource them?

Many engineers and executives are very talented within their niche. They are smart and some even enjoy considering their investment options. When it comes to outsourcing their investment management, they ask, "What is an advisor going to do for me that I can't do by myself?"

Long-term investing takes willpower, patience, and the ability to ignore shouts from the talking heads on cable TV. Unless you're a day trader, your investments are for future needs, such as lifestyle maintenance later in life. Any cash needed in the short term (less than five years) should not be invested in the stock market. The growth in your portfolio will allow you to achieve your goals far into the future, so you can continue to live just like you do now, with no reduction in spending or lifestyle.

The advisor who takes a personalized approach is looking at your situation continually, via your portfolio and your life, to guide you when you have a change in job, marital status, family status, and the like. A good advisor will be up to date on tax laws and investing tools and research—items that constantly change. If you are dedicated to your job, the only time you may have to focus on your portfolio is between 11 p.m. and 2 a.m., after you stop working for the day. Are you at your peak performance to be handling your financial future at that time? Can you be sure you'll take action when you need to, to trade in order to harvest tax losses, convert to a Roth IRA when your income is low (and the market may also be low, which feels like a scary time), or purchase adequate insurance to protect your net worth?

"From my perspective, why we hired an advisor is to look at it continually, not in a 2 to 4 a.m. window," says one recently retired executive.[24] The advisor is "looking at our situation and seeing what may be happening in the world, filtered to our particular situation. A Google search gives me a barrage of the top news stories for one topic, but without a customized filter."

Technologists are trained experts in a particular area, but they may not be able to answer detailed questions outside of their niche. The technical spectrum is only so wide for most people. Financial planning is equally nuanced. Your advisor should have a network of unbiased resources to help you. (However, be cautious of financial planners who tell you they can handle all of your needs—including insurance—in-house, as there may be conflicts of interest.)

With the right advisor, the benefits should outweigh the costs in management fees. However, if you have the time, interest, and skill set to manage your new wealth, then being your own financial planner might make sense.

If you're not sure where you fall on the DIY versus outsource spectrum, read on for tips to help you make an informed decision. And if you already know you don't want to spend the time or energy checking the markets daily and strategizing your financial life, turn to page 132 for guidance on partnering with a financial advisor and pages 176 to 180 for a guide to finding the right advisor.

CAN YOU DO YOUR OWN FINANCIAL PLANNING?

Online personal finance software, magazines, and self-help books claim to guide you in your financial planning. However, you may decide to seek help from a professional financial planner if:

- You lack expertise in certain areas of your financial picture, such as college savings plans, wealth protection, tax planning, charitable giving, or retirement projections due to changing family circumstances.
- You want a professional second opinion about the financial plan you have developed for yourself.
- You don't have the time to do your own financial planning.
- You have an immediate need for assistance, or an unexpected life event such as a birth, inheritance, or major illness.[25]

"The biggest pitfall" about personal financial management, says Yahoo CFO Ken Goldman, "is that you get overconfident. You don't create enough breathing room in your cash, so you go right to the cliff and you maybe jump off because you haven't [got enough]. I've seen people who just don't pay enough attention."

FIVE DECISIONS TO MAKE ABOUT INVESTING

In *The Investment Answer*, Daniel Goldie and Gordon Murray list five decisions you must make if you're thinking of taking charge of your own investing.[26] I've summarized each below and expanded on the rebalancing piece:

❶ **The Do-It-Yourself Decision.** Do you have the time and interest to manage your own finances? Does the money you save on professional management make up for the returns you may be missing out on?

❷ **The Asset Allocation Decision.** What percentage of volatile stocks to volatility-dampening bonds should you choose? How much downside can you handle on a day-to-day basis in order to meet your needs later in life? Are you aware of how to boost long-term returns, such as by adding small cap stocks and value stocks to your mix, which have historically outperformed large cap and growth stocks?

❸ **The Diversification Decision.** Holding many asset classes lowers your overall portfolio risk, and in most investing environments will protect you on the downside. How will you diversify?

❹ **The Active vs. Passive Decision.** Active management means using available information about the economy, specific industries, and companies to take advantage of mispriced stocks. Passive or index investing believes all available information is already reflected in the price of a stock. Which should you choose?

❺ **The Rebalancing Decision.** Since returns don't come nice and steady, asset classes in your portfolio will not move in lockstep. Independent of Goldie's view, research by Gobind Daryanani demonstrates that when an asset class moves outside of a 20% band higher or lower than the target set for that position, the trading fees are mitigated by the benefit of getting your portfolio back to target. (To understand the concept of a "band," think about a rubber band stretching, but not so far that it breaks. For example, if your target for large cap U.S. stocks is 30% and you have a 20% band, you would rebalance when the allocation drops below 24% or rises above 36%.)[27] The important principle here is to make time to review your portfolio for asset classes that have moved far beyond their targets, and pull the trigger to rebalance.

HOW TO BE YOUR OWN FINANCIAL PLANNER: IMPLEMENT, MONITOR & ACT

As a wealth planner devoted to helping my clients make smart choices and achieve their dreams, I believe that everyone can benefit from the services of an advisor, even if it's just for a yearly checkup. But if you're a DIY person, you may want to be your own financial planner.

If so, make sure you carve out enough time on a quarterly basis, at least (or a daily basis, if you hold individual stocks), to review and research investments, monitor your holdings, add surplus cash to your portfolio, and rebalance as needed. Write down your life goals, including the cost and the time period of any expense. Then, annually review and update your goals to make sure that your priorities reflect any changes in your life. It's important to follow through on action items in a timely manner. Being your own financial planner requires you to look at the big picture as well as the details, to keep yourself on track to achieve your goals.

While research[28] shows that working with an impartial, knowledgeable financial professional can set you and your family up for greater success—financial and otherwise—for the rest of your life, it is possible to go it alone. In fact, an early Google employee says this about the many brilliant engineers she knows who are investing DIYers: "I think a lot of them actually do a fine job."[29] They read a few publications or do web research and "put their dollars in a diversified portfolio, and they go ahead and let it ride. It might not be optimized, it might not be as much [as they could earn with an advisor], but it's hard to tell what would have been." The ex-Googler, who uses an advisor herself, paraphrases these DIYers: "I'd rather know what I know and have myself make the mistakes, rather than pay someone X dollars, when I don't know how much better they would have been able to do."

I know the type. My engineer brother talks to me about his stocks and mutual funds on holidays and summer vacations. He knows about the benefits of tax loss harvesting but doesn't make the time to actively review his portfolio on a regular basis. One year, I happened to see him just before the last trading day of a particularly volatile year for stocks. We got to talking about the losses in his portfolio, and I suggested that he realize the tax loss on paper by selling a handful of funds before the end of the year. He did, but without prompting from me, he would have lost that opportunity—and the thousands of dollars in taxes it saved him.

EVAN'S STORY
TOO BUSY CREATING COMPANIES TO CREATE A PLAN OF HIS OWN.

"I just don't have time to tax plan," says Evan,[30] a high-tech executive who was recently part of an acquisition. "I work 20 hours a day. And so to me, to spend any amount of time outside of that focused on optimizing dollars is really ridiculous. That's because I have the philosophy that I have to enjoy my life. I don't want to lose sleep over worrying about dollars and cents, if I know that what I have done so far has worked and it's getting me a return that I'm happy with. So putting my money in mutual funds is easy for me. I keep some in cash so that I know I can pay for that big credit card bill when I go on vacation. But basically that's it."

Evan may think he's got a winning strategy. He's working hard, enjoying life, investing a little, and keeping up his cash reserves in a way that doesn't stress him out. But he could be making huge financial mistakes without even realizing it. Mutual funds can be a smart piece of anyone's investment mix, but they are rarely the only piece in a wise financial plan.

Here are a handful of questions I would ask Evan. The answers can have a huge impact on his life—and his finances.

- You say you're putting away some money, but how do you know you're saving enough for retirement?
- Do you have enough insurance?
- How do you know if the mutual funds you're buying are generating the best returns? Are your funds diversified? What if there are other funds with the same fees and risk level that

are better for you?

- Do you want to pay more than your fair share in taxes?
- Will your family be OK if you die, get sued, lose your job, or get sick?
- Will your money, property, and other assets go quickly where you want them to go if you die or become incapacitated?

As life gets more complicated, an advisor can offer Evan and others in his boat the following:

- **Peace of Mind**—The confidence of knowing you have a plan to achieve your goals.
- **Accountability**—A resource who will hold you responsible for implementing your financial plan.
- **A Savings Target**—Ensure that you are saving enough today to achieve your goals and maintain your lifestyle in retirement.
- **Tax and Money Savings**—Guidance for how to take advantage of tax breaks, avoid inappropriate or excessive insurance, and invest in a tax-efficient, low-cost, risk-appropriate manner.
- **Fast-Track Goal Achievement**—Reach your goals faster by ensuring that you're not wasting money on overpriced or unnecessary financial products, and that your investments are growing in the most efficient way possible.

The Accidental Do-It-Yourselfer

During the Great Recession of 2008 and early 2009, I had a client who had neither the interest nor the time to devote to the management of his family's financial affairs. He is smart and financially savvy, holding an MBA from the Kellogg School at Northwestern University, one of the top-ranked business schools in the United States. The client worked in the corporate finance department of a Fortune 500 company. As he was responsible for making short-term economic forecasts for his employer, he had a hard time de-linking his extremely negative short-term forecasts from the long-term focus needed for his investment portfolio during the weak economic environment. He was only 50 and wanted to stop working at 55, meaning he could be looking at a good 40 years in retirement.

The client sent me weekly emails to explain the three- to nine-month economic forecasts he was making for his company. He was eager to preserve his wealth, so keeping him invested took a lot of education—and conversation. Ultimately, he was not able to delegate when the investment waters got too rough, and he sold his holdings near the bottom of the bear market. Sadly, he missed the big returns that the stock market saw in 2009 and subsequent years. The bottom line is that like many proponents of passive investing, I believe stock prices already reflect all available information. Additionally, no one can consistently time the market.

This accidental DIYer learned his lesson the hard way.

Returns of DIY Investors

Every year, DALBAR conducts research to assess how well the average investor did versus the benchmark. Sadly, the average investor's return in some cases didn't beat inflation, which averaged 2.5% annualized during this time period.

The "Annualized Investor Returns Versus Benchmarks" chart (Figure 6) provides a good snapshot of the disappointing performance individual investors experience. From 1990 to 2011, the average investor saw an astoundingly low 3.49% annualized return. Over that same time frame, the S&P 500 returned 7.81%.[31] Many bond investors realized similar underperformance: the average bond investor earned 0.9%, while the bond index earned 6.5% annualized over more than two decades. For the 21-year period ending December 31, 2011, both equity and fixed income mutual fund investors underperformed the market for every time frame.[32] This situation was likely due to investors trying to time the market. If you managed your own portfolio, it's likely you did much worse than if you just bought the index and held on for the long term.

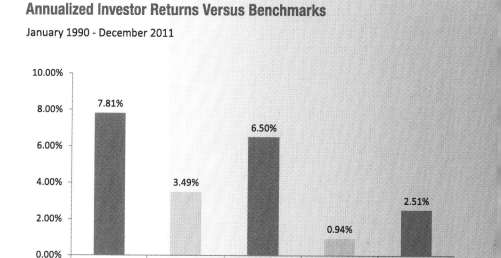

Figure 6. Annualized investor returns versus benchmarks for the 21-year period ending December 31, 2011.[33]

New research from Morningstar shows that compared to a DIY investor, the added value of financial planning can be an extra 1.82% per year to investment returns. Morningstar quantified how much additional retirement income investors can generate by making better financial planning decisions, a measurement Morningstar calls "Gamma." In addition to picking good investments, "good financial-planning decisions are very important to success," says David Blanchett, the head of retirement research for Morningstar Investment Management.[34] "It's hard to quantify the benefit someone receives from someone who gives good financial advice. Gamma is the idea that there is more to just helping someone than picking good funds."

As a CPA who has helped hundreds of people in startups and high-tech companies create plans with their stock options, former Oracle CFO Roy Bukstein believes people who use a third-party advisor to handle their financial affairs have a success rate of 8 on a scale of 1 to 10, with 10 being the most successful. But he gives do-it-yourselfers only a 5 for effectiveness. He cautions people to take a "long-term view. You can't look at it as a short-term [event]. It's a marathon, so choose [your advisor] wisely," says Bukstein.

Consider your own responses to these questions: Where do you get your most important information? Do you get it from the media or directly from experts? "What you read in a publication is either static, or historic," says one source. "There's very little projecting the future, [because it] is very hard to do. [Media outlets] always look backwards and it's always [at] the negative stuff. And [the major TV networks are] narrow-minded, not global. When we get our news, we don't have the big picture."

Partnering with a Financial Advisor

Many executives who reflect upon their interests and understand their short-comings early on can get the right help by outsourcing to an advisor who possesses the skills or time they lack. By Phase 3, you already know how to play great offense: you successfully managed risk and parlayed it into real wealth. Now is the time to implement a great defense in order to make your wealth last.

The great defense that an advisor offers is to help you avoid too much risk while guiding you to accept what risk you need to stay ahead of inflation, making sure you're saving enough for the future, ensuring that you have adequate asset protection, giving you clear direction, and identifying any gaps that may exist in your plan. The special value an advisor provides is not telling you the 10 best mutual funds; it's preventing you from making mistakes with your wealth, such as bailing out of the market in the depths of the 2008/2009 Great Recession. Following the recommendations of a smart, ethical advisor will help you save your financial life by making sure you don't make big—but sadly, common—mistakes.

GUIDANCE FROM YOUR PERSONAL CFO

Ideally, your financial planning partner will advise you on more than just investments. Your planner should understand your goals (and review them at every meeting), analyze the resources available to achieve those goals, implement and monitor your asset allocation, and provide specific, actionable instructions for issues outside of his/her direct management. For example, a wise planner can recommend a specific amount of life insurance and offer guidance on asset protection and tax minimization. He or she should provide referrals to professionals to assist you in completing the recommendations.

As your personal financial manager, a planner sees your complete picture. Are you taking unnecessary financial risks? Do you have protection from creditors and others who may try to tap the hard-earned wealth you've worked so hard to build and protect? (The solution to that particular issue could be umbrella liability insurance.) A planner should ask good questions and have meaningful conversations to better understand what's important to you.

Ultimately, outsourcing the management of your personal finances brings you a level of technical competence and expertise about financial management that's similar to what you bring to your career or company. Your advisor should be an extra set of eyes on this important piece of your life; working with a professional forces you to attend to financial affairs. And of course, what you focus on grows.

CAN YOU DIVERSIFY BY ADVISOR?

Some people falsely believe diversification means spreading your assets among several advisors or institutions. While this tactic seems safe, you may actually be doubling up on the same holdings, or buying expensive investments where a lower-cost alternative (often with higher returns) exists. In fact, multiple accounts at different custodians add costs and potential tax inefficiencies that hinder growth, and having assets at many companies could lead to a nightmare for your heirs in the event of your premature death.

OUTSOURCING FINANCIAL MANAGEMENT

Hiring an advisor is a really big step that requires a great deal of research and forethought. Not only must you be confident in the advisor's expertise, knowledge, and follow-through, but you also need to be able to connect and communicate with the advisor.

Marc Tarpenning, a serial entrepreneur who now acts as a consultant to startups while waiting for his next big thing to come along, says, "Over the years as these liquidity events have happened, frequently I end up thinking, 'Well, what am I going to do with this money?'" He chooses to outsource to a professional to manage it. "As much as I love economics, and I love the micro-picture, I don't get that much out of the minutiae." Tarpenning adds, "I want them to not lose money. I want to just sit there on autopilot and [have my advisor] keep everything going along so that I can do the things that I want to do. I don't want a lot of interaction with them. As long as things are rocking along," he's happy. And when it's time to fund an angel investment or his own company, "I just want the money to be available. I want to be able to say, I'm going to need $100,000 in the next week, because we're going to make an investment."

Many entrepreneurs get big checks every once in a while. Then, there are long periods when no cash comes in. With one of his big checks, Tarpenning carved out a chunk to put into 529s (tax-free college savings plans) for his three children, so "at least I know that college is not going to bankrupt us."

Others outsource their wealth planning to free up time for what they love. For many entrepreneurs and executives profiled in this book, what they love is not managing their finances, but creating companies and spending time with their family.

Focus on Building a Business

Jeff Russakow, who holds a PhD in mechanical engineering from Stanford, explains his attitude toward his own personal finances like this: "I know my personality well enough to know I can run and grow a multibillion-dollar business—I love building the valuation of a company—but I don't like managing money. I don't have the discipline to look at my portfolio holdings every day."[35] In addition to discipline, he believes that being a successful investor requires an objectivity that is hard for an entrepreneur or operator to maintain. "If you're someone who builds businesses, you tend to join a team. You're on a mission for years and you have a goal to move one stock. So you genetically and emotionally don't have the discipline to be a great investor, because that's just not how you operate. You do not have good discipline around when to sell, you tend to hold things too long."

As a team-focused company cheerleader in Phases 1 and 2, Russakow says, "You get excited about your company, you focus on your job 110%, and you don't even look at your [company's] market valuation for months at a crack." At that point, "Most of your wealth is usually on paper that you can't liquidate yet. So you're not worried about managing that wealth, just maximizing the value of your company." After the liquidity event, "Suddenly the money shows up and you're like, well I don't really know what to do with it. I'm not very good at actively managing wealth, and don't have a passion or discipline for it. I have little experience as an investor. And I am on to my next exciting job or company." He acknowledges that the best way to achieve his goals is to turn over the day-to-day management of his portfolio to "somebody who is going to actively manage it for me who understands" how financial markets operate and what his family's goals are.

Most executives post-liquidity know they should invest their windfall in a diversified portfolio. However, as Russakow explains, "The issue is they don't actually do it. It's not a priority. They put more time into their next project." His advice? "Decide on an investment strategy. Then, find the time or the person to execute on it well."

One engineer who has had three successful liquidity events told me the following: "Through the years, I have certainly had employees who have gotten themselves into trouble by exercising options [and holding the company stock], not thinking through when they were going to have to pay taxes. Entrepreneurs aren't thought of as conservative. But when it comes to [financial] planning, I have always solicited advice and have understood what was going on."[36]

Even VC Lara Druyan, a former investment banker, outsources part of her financial management. This fact surprises her friends and colleagues who say, "You know so much. How come you're not doing it all yourself?"

"Because I work and I have children," she answers. Smartly, she acknowledges that "unless you're going to devote a significant time and you really know what you're doing, [not outsourcing is] kind of nutty. Because the reason I have someone watching over some of the stuff for me is I just don't have the time." She knows holding on to what she has is about effectively managing it. "People really get fleeced," if they don't protect their hard-earned wealth.

Financial Tune-Ups

Tech workers in a startup often put in 20 hours a day, and several I interviewed told me they did not have time or interest to focus on their personal finances. In a way, that's a good thing, because after a liquidity event, managing your own portfolio without a written plan could put your hard-won windfall at risk. On the other hand, some of my sources are DIYers who believe they have the time, temperament, interest, and cautious (but not too cautious) nature to tackle their finances alone.

If, after reading *The Investment Answer* decisions earlier in this chapter—or uncovering your skills, preferences, and weaknesses in other ways—you decide that you're a do-it-yourself investor, consider meeting once a year with an advisor for a tune-up. Find a financial planner who works on an hourly basis, someone you can see as much or as little as you need, possibly only a few hours a year. The planner can review your situation—over and above investments—and provide recommendations for you to act on.

However, if you've decided to outsource to an advisor, consult my guide to finding the right financial planner for you on page 177.

Whether a professional is involved just a few hours a year, or every day of the year, another benefit a professional set of eyes can confer is a reality check about investing in unfamiliar areas or overspending. The next profile explores how a tech entrepreneur with $200 million was forced to declare bankruptcy in just five years.

consult my guide to finding the right financial planner for you on page 177.

PROFILE
A TECH ICON CRUMBLES: HALSEY MINOR

CNET'S CO-FOUNDER STRAYED FROM HIS EXPERTISE AND BLEW THROUGH $200 MILLION.

In 1999, the world was Halsey Minor's oyster: he was the CEO of C|net Inc. (CNET), valued at more than $3 billion, and lived with his wife and three children in San Francisco's Seacliff neighborhood in a house overlooking the Pacific Ocean and the Golden Gate Bridge.[37] But 14 years later, Minor declared bankruptcy under the weight of a

$100 million debt that his approximately $50 million in assets could not come close to matching, according to Bloomberg.[38]

What Went Wrong?

Perhaps Minor became overconfident after his amazing success, leading him to make real estate investments, large fine art purchases, and angel investments without having a coordinated spending and cash flow plan.

From an early age, Minor was attracted to the high-tech world. As a teen, he attended the all-male, private Woodberry Forest High School, citing its computer lab as his main reason for choosing the school.[39]

After graduating from college with a degree in anthropology, Minor co-founded CNET, one of the first ventures in online technology news. CNET went public in 1999 and was acquired in 2008 by CBS Corporation for $1.8 billion, of which Minor took home $200 million.[40] These were not Minor's only successes. His firm, Minor Ventures, which invested in early-stage tech and media startups, was well rewarded when one of its portfolio companies, GrandCentral Communications Inc., was bought by Google in 2007 for $65 million and later renamed Google Voice.[41]

But those risky wins couldn't continue forever, and Minor invited significant losses when he stepped too far out of his technology comfort zone. According to the *Daily Progress*, Minor said, "I like doing things outside my comfort zone, and I believe that willingness in part accounts for my tech successes."[42] For $15.3 million, Minor bought the Carter's Grove Plantation, an 18th-century mansion on 400-plus acres, with the intention of raising racehorses and keeping up the estate.[43] Around the same time in 2008, he was also building a hotel in Charlottesville, Virginia, under the moniker Minor Family Hotels LLC, and accumulating a personal art collection.

In 2010, Minor was forced to file for bankruptcy for the ill-fated hotel company, and Carter's Grove filed for bankruptcy protection in 2011.[44] Scrambling to pay his debts, Minor began selling his prized art for tens of millions of dollars.[45] In May 2013, he declared personal bankruptcy, listing assets of $32 million and debt of more than $100 million.[46]

What can be learned from Minor's rise and fall? Although his adventurous mind contributed to early prosperity, something went awry when he invested so heavily into ventures in less familiar fields. Expensive hobbies and major capital investments should be part of a coordinated wealth plan.

Unfortunately, Silicon Valley is filled with less well-known versions of Halsey Minor's story, in which people lost smaller fortunes because they didn't plan or thought they could manage their finances themselves.

By now, you should have a plan for your money. But do you have a plan for your life?

Getting Back in the Game

After a liquidity event, many people take time off, if only to find their next venture or job. Taking a company to a successful exit is exhilarating, but it also requires a great deal of mental and physical energy. You may not have to get up in the morning and work right away, but do consider the length of your break, depending on the size of the exit and how you define success.

"The top line issue is, how long are you going to be absent before you get back into the game again?" says attorney Mark Cameron White. "The companies and entrepreneurs that I work with generally don't go off into the sunset and find charitable activities and things to do that are not related to how they made their money in the first place. . . . Everybody in the Valley wants to be in the game. Forever. In one way or another. Most of these guys are trying to figure out how to come up with the next big idea or to get involved in companies as mentors, to be active participants. The people I work with aren't figuring out how to spend their money. What they do is they don't spend it. They salt it away."

Discussing a thrice-successful entrepreneur who is now taking time off from building his own company, White explains the man's new role at a venture capital firm as "looking at everything that's coming into that firm. He's going to cherry-pick what he wants to be associated with and then he's going to [invest in] that. What he's doing is he's putting himself in a position where opportunities are coming to him, and he's going to figure out what he wants to do."

It's tricky, says White, "because your skill set becomes pretty antiquated really fast in this community. I can't speak about Kansas, but here, if you're out of it for six months, the world changes. The folks that are important change, the sectors that are emerging and becoming more interesting change, relationships get stale." In response to this issue, White offers a time-off timeline: "The younger you are, the transition period is shorter. If you're in your 50s, it's 24 months. If you're in your 40s, it's 12 months. If you are in your 30s, it's three to six months. Is it linear? No. But in broad parameters, probably yes. The reason is, it's not just business. It's also about your family obligations. If you're in your late 30s or early 40s, you've got children that are 5 to 12 years old, so you're going to pay attention to them. In Phase 1, when you built the company, you were not around; you want to make up for lost time." Yet, taking off just 12 months could leave you feeling like a fish out of water.

When asked if she's known or heard of any of her peers in their 20s or 30s who just hang out or travel after a liquidity event, former Director of Business Development at Tiny Prints Sylvia Yam says, "No. Not a single person. There's probably some version of it, like maybe their family came from a great amount of success, and they've always lived an easy lifestyle. But I feel like anyone who is an entrepreneur, at least in this area or this community, is very likely to just go back to work. Or seek an idea or do a passion project," such as charitable involvement.

Reflecting on patterns he's seen over 30 years as both an advisor and then a serial entrepreneur, John Bowen agrees that successful high-tech executives "don't retire. They write next chapters."

CREATIVITY IN TIME OFF: SANTOSH SHARAN

SOLD KEISENSE IN 2010 TO NUANCE COMMUNICATIONS.

Santosh Sharan is intensely curious. Born in India, he earned a Harvard engineering degree and an MBA from the London Business School. His company, Keisense, developed predictive technologies to enhance input and search experience in mobile devices. The company generated over 16 patents and was acquired by Nuance Communications in 2010. Like many entrepreneurs, Sharan gives his all to his startups. In each company, he says, "Building one solution required a lot of focus. You get very good at what you are doing, but then you lose track of the rest of the world." His antidote to the chaos of a startup is a long break during which his creative juices flow.

For Sharan, the real prize is the three to six months of downtime after each exit. His pace goes from crazy to lazy: he reads books, explores what's happening in other fields, watches movies, catches up with family, and travels.

During one extended work break, Sharan returned to his homeland and spent three months in a Himalayan village where he knew no one. He passed the time appreciating the natural beauty, watching the stars, "meeting random people," and naturally getting creative. "I really found that time quite precious," he remembers of this period away from day-to-day life and his wife and children back home in Massachusetts.

In one Indian city, he noticed consistently long lines of people next to each ATM. It turns out people in India don't trust the ATM receipts, so after withdrawing money, they take their bank passbook and stand in a queue to have it updated by a live person with a printer. "It didn't make any sense," remembers Sharan, "so I got a friend to build a kiosk that you could put next to the ATM." Identifying and building a solution to the cultural needs of the country's citizens was easy for native Sharan. Two years after starting that 40-person Bangalore company, annual revenues are $1.5 million.

Sharan tells me about many other ideas he's researched, ranging from entertainment (renting movies on tablet PCs for passengers on low-cost Asian airlines—Bollywood aggregators made it difficult to close content licensing deals, and the airlines have since implemented the program themselves), gift giving (Regaalo, a website aimed at parents of college students), energy, and health care. "I just look for opportunities wherever I go," says Sharan.

After each post-exit break, as the clock ticks closer to the six-month mark, Sharan begins to ramp back up and networks in the community to find a new team to join him for his next Phase 1 journey.

Reflecting on his creative breaks, Sharan concludes, "I value my time a lot. . . . I see this as a journey without any destination." He lives life seeking meaning and positive impact through his companies and his employees. "I just enjoy it. For good or for bad, this is who I am."

Most entrepreneurs don't stay out of the game for long. Instead, they start another company, get involved with boards and consulting, or switch to angel investing.

Angel Investing Motivation, Tips & Overconfidence

A popular way to stay involved in the action post-liquidity event is to become an angel investor or work with accelerators (startup incubators). Some like the bragging rights of being involved in creating cool technology—as well as the chance to make money at it. But most just love the excitement of building companies, creating products, and cultivating new ideas without the grueling 16-hour workdays that accompany launching their own startups.

While Peter Herz currently focuses on entrepreneurial endeavors, longer term he aims to continue participating in a number of projects into his 60s and 70s. He intends to serve as "an advisor or in a board capacity, and keep plugged in but not in the day-to-day management of companies." In 10 or 20 years, through angel investing, he can stay involved in what he loves—"learning about a new business area, new concepts, new issues that companies have"—without the pressures of operating in the daily grind.

To Stephen Roth, a software development entrepreneur, angel investing can feed both his ego and the aspirations of his wallet: "We [as entrepreneurs] can relate to the struggles, and I want to help out. But of course I'm not doing it as a charity case. I'm doing it because I also want to succeed and make money."[47] Finally, some feel invincible after their first success. They did so well with their own company, they assume they'll have another big win if they invest in a promising startup.

OPPORTUNITIES ARE EVERYWHERE

"Startup companies generally do not need as much capital to get going nowadays as before,"[48] says Darrell Kong, former Director of Venture Capital Services at Fenwick & West, a technology and life sciences law firm.[49] "A new class of investors has come up. These are a lot of Facebook and Google [early] employees who have gotten liquidity events." Angel investing is a popular activity for these folks, says Kong, in part because "the amount of money that early stage companies have to raise is a lot less now."

"If you've had a liquidity event, most likely you have a network of people you've worked with, people you trust," says VC and ex-investment banker Lara Druyan. "The great thing about Silicon Valley is there are always new companies starting up. You end up besieged by opportunities to invest in little companies."

Druyan explains the importance of looking at new companies and seeing what's hot—so that even if you're not "employed" full-time by your previous company, or by a new startup, you can continue to practice your craft and stay current as an investor, especially in the ever-changing tech world. Other reasons Druyan gives for angel investing? "Because [the founders are] friends of yours, because you're helping and advising, because you're keeping current, or because you may decide that you want to join one of these" companies one day. After people have been successful, they feel like they may have something to impart to other people, including lessons learned, functional expertise, and industry expertise.

Angel and VC Investment Definitions

Investors finance startups at various stages. Early funding opportunities are usually found by tapping your network for referrals and by attending industry events.

SEED MONEY

Seed money is generally the first round of startup capital and the riskiest investment, because the startup is young and often has only an untested idea. Often, seed money comes from personal savings of the founders, or from founders' friends and family (playfully termed FFF, or "friends, family, and fools"). Some venture capital firms reserve a small amount of money for seed investing. Seed investors are compensated with equity (shares or stock options) in the company.[50]

ANGEL INVESTORS

Angel investors often bridge the funding gap between seed investments and venture capital. Typically, an angel investment is in the $250,000 to $500,000 range,[51] although it may actually be much lower. While technically anyone can make an angel investment, startups are advised to look for accredited investors who satisfy SEC standards: individuals must have a net worth of more than $1 million, excluding their primary residence.[52] Angels often work alone, though angel groups who pool resources to make investments are becoming more popular. After making an investment, angels may serve in advisory roles, coaching the company toward an exit such as an acquisition or IPO.

VENTURE CAPITALISTS

Venture capitalists are similar to angel investors in the way they invest, but they don't work on the day-to-day operations. VCs generally invest larger amounts in the later stages of startup funding, while angels will invest smaller amounts earlier (see chart below). VCs, like angels, often act in a guidance capacity. Unlike angels, venture capitalists work primarily through a venture capital fund, gathering assets from many investors who share in the fund's profits, including both individual investors and larger institutions and pension funds, such as CalPERS and other large retirement funds.[53]

Equity Capital Markets: Angel & VC Investment

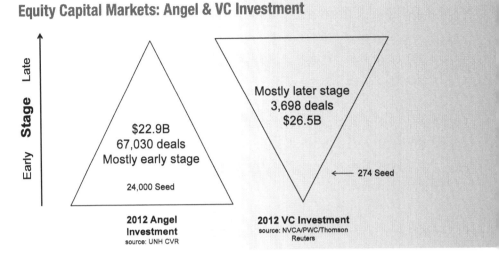

Figure 7. A comparison of angel and VC investment markets.[54]

FUNDING

The different stages of investment are formally called the seed stage, series A round, series B round, and series C round, with additional letters as needed.

In the seed stage, companies look for the initial capital they need for product development. Here, they may file for patents, conduct market surveys, and look to recruit business partners.

In the series A round, the startup should be ready to begin operations, if it hasn't begun already. The startup may be seeing its first revenues during series A, and this is usually the first time companies bring in outside investors.

Series B funding is used to grow the business, allowing the company to hire more staff and enact a marketing plan. Between series B and series C funding, startups can also start looking to commercial banks for a line of credit. At this point, the company typically makes plans to be acquired or to IPO.

When companies enter series C rounds, they start to expand more rapidly. Again, they may look for outside investments, hoping to become a presence in their industry and make enough noise to satisfy the investors' liquidity goals.[55]

Start Slowly

"My advice would be don't start with an angel investment," urges Nicolai Wadstrom,[56] who runs startup accelerator BootstrapLabs. "It's the first time, so that's when you're going to make all the mistakes. Usually people—myself included—[tend to be] a little bit too sure of themselves because of their recent success, and you throw money away too easily without fully understanding the dynamics behind it."

He doesn't warn against angel investments entirely, but advises novice angels to do their homework first, because the risks are so high. Wadstrom says, "Start to leverage the skills you have as an advisor. Find a couple of startups and entrepreneurs, and work for a bit alongside them. Then, start to do angel investments, maybe into the same companies, because then you'll be able to understand what skills you have to assess these things, and how you can bring value to make things more likely to succeed. At that point, it's much easier to assess what things you should be in, and what things you should not be into."

Angel Investing Success:
Time, Experience & Participation

Research conducted by the Kauffman Foundation supports Wadstrom's suggestions.[57] The report found three areas angel investors should focus on to increase their chances of a positive return: time in due diligence, industry experience, and participation with the portfolio companies.

The more time angels spend in due diligence before investing, the higher the returns they can expect. The table below shows the results of the time factor.

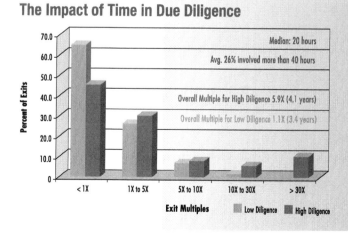

Figure 8. The impact of time in due diligence, as seen in the percent of exits and exit multiples in research conducted by the Kauffman Foundation. (Wadhwa et al.; *The Anatomy of an Entrepreneur: Making of a Successful Entrepreneur.*)

Angel investors who conducted less than the median number of hours (20) of due diligence only received 1.1X of what they put into the company. Conversely, those who conducted greater than 20 hours enjoyed a return 5.9X on their initial investment. The top quartile, who spent more than 40 hours on due diligence, had an average return of 7.1X their outlay. Familiarity with the industry has similarly positive results. Though half the investments made in the study were outside of an angel's industry, investment return multiples were two times higher for those with industry experience than for those without.

Frequent interaction with portfolio companies had a similar effect on an angel's returns. Angels who participated—via mentoring or coaching, strategic consultation, and monitoring of financial information—in their venture companies a couple of times a month saw 3.7X returns in four years, while those who only checked in a couple of times a year had overall multiples of 1.3X. Of course, as the frequency of participation increases, the quality of the interaction becomes more important.

The Kauffman Foundation study implies two warnings: First, follow-on (repeat) investments can be tricky. Angels who make follow-on investments tend to experience lower returns, and 68% of exits that took a follow-on investment resulted in a loss for the investor. On the other hand, sometimes that investment can be the factor that saves a startup, and companies that took follow-on investments still had a positive average return of 1.4X. (Those that do not need follow-on investments have an average return of 3.6X.) The second red flag for failure is putting all your eggs in one basket and staking your financial future on the success of one or two companies. Since 48% of all exits returned more than what the angel invested, 52%—more than half—returned less than the original investment.[58]

The VC or angel funding world often "looks glamorous from the outside" to tech community members, says VC and professor Brendan Richardson. It's "the place where, as an investor, you are at the intersection of ideas, technology, and creativity/innovation," he explains. "VCs are really investing in imagination," and they're excited and fulfilled by helping to develop world-changing ideas. "That's the fantasy we all want to participate in, to be able to change the world and be at the nexus—at that crucible of innovation—early on."

However, Richardson reminds us, "Failure is by far the more likely outcome in the startup world than an Instagram-like success."

Risks in Angel Investing

Whatever your reason for becoming an angel investor, there are real risks involved. Dr. Scott A. Shane, a professor of entrepreneurial studies at Case Western Reserve University and author of *Fool's Gold: The Truth Behind Angel Investing in America*, explains the low odds of success in an interview with *Failure* magazine. "Less than 0.2% of angel-backed companies end in an IPO, and less than 1.5% end in an acquisition." Shane continues, "40% of the investments return less money than the capital that goes in," while only "7% of the investments account for 75% of all returns. It's the few phenomenal outcomes that make up for the losses of most." He stresses that it's important to be realistic. "If you think the typical angel investment is going to return an internal rate of return of 30% per year, you are going to be very disappointed unless you are really lucky."[59]

Darrell Kong, who worked as an advisor to many early-stage companies, says many startups "take the Google approach and throw something out there before it's fully baked and see what happens. There's a little bit of survival of the fittest. Some of those companies are going to hit their stride and raise that next round of money, but a lot of them don't. If they've raised half a million dollars from angels, and they need more money to sustain what these angels really aren't able to do," the investors who have already committed are in a difficult position when the startup needs more cash. "If things don't happen," continues Kong, "and the exit opportunities that everyone's been hoping for aren't there, then things start backing up." At that point, the company must either swim (raise more money) or sink (and the angel investors lose their investment).[60]

Kong explains that if a liquidity event does not happen, there are no exits for the investors, and the startup must "keep these things alive on life support." He asks, "When these [angel-financed] companies start coming back to the well needing three or four million dollars, and I haven't seen any exits in the meantime, am I willing to keep doing that?"

INCUBATOR AND ANGEL INVESTOR: NICOLAI WADSTROM

ACCELERATED MORE THAN $250 MILLION IN STARTUP VALUATION BETWEEN 2009 AND 2013.[61]

By the time he was 15 years old, Nicolai Wadstrom was already a successful entrepreneur. He was living in Sweden and running a profitable programming and software startup that enabled him to support his coding hobby.

Fulfilling His Passion: Living in Phases 1 and 2

Wadstrom's interest in angel investing stems from his desire to mentor: "For me, angel investment wasn't about building a lot of wealth," he explains. "It was a way for me to pursue the passion of entrepreneurship." Wadstrom started his accelerator, BootstrapLabs, so he could stay in Phase 1, his favorite part of building companies. "I like the intensity. I'm very driven by working with other people. I really like the environment where I come in and actually help drive the process with a team of smart, great entrepreneurs," he says. "I never wanted to pursue this passive angel investment, 'here's a check, and I'll come and look at how things are going in a couple of months, or a year.'"

Since successful companies grow out of Phases 1 and 2, the accelerator was a brilliant way to constantly stay in these phases with a handful of companies at one time.

A Systematic Approach to Angel Investing

Beginning in 2006, after several liquidity events of his own, Wadstrom started using a portion of his money for angel investments. He explains that while a big return on investment would be nice, his real passion is seeing the success of those he has mentored.

His journey has taken him from Sweden to London to the Bay Area, through various business partnerships and inside many companies—both as an owner and as a mentor. His path led him to start BootstrapLabs. "I wanted to build this platform to do advisory and investment work," says Wadstrom, using "the repetitive patterns and recognitions needed to make [a successful business] work over time." He uses his broad experience and a few close advisors to help startups identify patterns, which are then addressed within BootstrapLabs.

While he believes he has a structured approach to building a startup, Wadstrom echoes other sources for this book when he says surprises always happen. "Very little is predetermined. Everything's a surprise, so expect everything." As such, he takes a cautious and thoughtful approach: "The companies come into BootstrapLabs. I work with them a little bit, get to know the entrepreneurs. And then I would invest at some point when I actually know a lot more about the people and the startup."

Failure to Preserve Capital for Your Future

Wadstrom told me a sad story about a good friend back in Sweden. As the co-founder of a successful company, at one point during the dot-com bubble the friend was worth $1 billion. But he invested in too many businesses, such as restaurants, movies, and gaming cafes, and "burned too much too quickly." The friend didn't segregate a "Maintain" reserve of cash and prudent investments to carry him through, and he didn't realize that a stable reserve would provide for him and his family, irrespective of the success or failure of his future entrepreneurial endeavors. "All those investments turned into nothing," Wadstrom recalls.

What truly upsets Wadstrom is to see friends unable to pursue entrepreneurial endeavors because they burned through cash on investments that became worthless. A better way for newly successful entrepreneurs to angel invest, advises Wadstrom, is to "pick one thing. Be prepared to lose the money on that, but make sure you learn something. If you can't find that thing that you understand and have the passion for, wait until you do."

Creating a Personal Freedom Platform

After the first liquidity event, says Wadstrom, "your focus shifts a bit," and you spend a lot of time thinking about how "to create a platform for personal freedom." Understand what must be in place to provide you with income for your lifestyle needs. And, just as important, address the question of how to deploy the rest of your cash after carving out a Maintain Bucket.

Wadstrom encourages entrepreneurs to find out "how to make a difference that you're passionate about." Now that you have more choices about how to spend your time, "you're able to actually make something that matters. If that is mentoring entrepreneurs, if that is angel investments, whatever. But something that you can [do to] make a difference. Find something you're passionate about."

Financial Advice for Serial Entrepreneurs

After the second entrepreneurial success, managing wealth "becomes quite different," Wadstrom explains. "If you've done it once, you know, build the platform. If that's what you want to continue to do, make sure you plan for that." Whatever your personal passion is—creating another company, for example—make sure you can maintain your personal financial freedom with a portion of the wealth you've created. "If you can get $100,000 to $200,000 a year in [portfolio] returns, you can live pretty well even in the expensive Bay Area. You always have something to fall back on, and that creates tremendous freedom to pick what you want to do."

Echoing my three-bucket formula for preserving capital, Wadstrom advises entrepreneurs who've had a liquidity event to "divide the cash into different baskets. Have something that gives you a certain return to create freedom for you to work [doing] what you want." Your Maintain portfolio will provide an annual return for you to live on for a long, long time. "And then you put a little bit on the back end for freedom, [but] limit the amount of play money, and don't deploy it all at once. Really try to figure out things you know well, that you're really passionate about." He then cautions, "I think you should just be very slow on figuring out what to do. Or you should have a really clear view of how you can deploy the cash and invest into things that make sense and matter to you."

Family Time

I met Wadstrom, who speaks five languages, over Skype; he was in Sweden for the summer, spending time with his wife, two daughters, and extended family. He had just introduced his infant daughter to his mom, who was thrilled to bond with her granddaughters.

Stories and advice rolled off his tongue, and I realized that physical distance couldn't unplug Wadstrom from the startup world for too long. It's a good thing he is enjoying time with his children now. As an entrepreneur, he's always trying to get back to Phase 1. Just as companies grow out of Phase 2 and have a liquidity event, his children will graduate from childhood one day. Perhaps having grandchildren will feel similar to returning to the early phases of a business's life cycle; only time will tell.

In the meantime, this super-connected member of the startup community has a strategized personal investment plan and is living his passions by mentoring and investing in others who hope to follow in his footsteps.

Your Angel Investing Policy: How Much to Invest?

Many of those I interviewed made small investments in a number of different companies, ideally carving out a discrete pot of angel investment funds in a "Risk" portfolio, and never handing over money they need to sustain their lifestyle.

Entrepreneur Rob Nail addresses the "How much?" question by dividing his acquisition proceeds into sections and keeping "a chunk of money that you're not going to lose sitting aside somewhere else." I call this the "Maintain Bucket," meant for your long-term security. As Nail explains it, his strategy is to segregate his Risk assets for things like angel investments, and then "not do any more than that."

A great way to increase your investing discipline is to have a written plan. For example, Nicolai Wadstrom limits himself to an annual budget of three startups at $10,000 to $100,000 each. Earmarking funds before you start angel investing can help you avoid putting your total net worth at risk.

Most entrepreneurs eventually start another company after their liquidity event. Just as it's tempting to assume success in angel investing, caution is advised with your net worth if you decide to start another company.

HOPING THAT LIGHTNING STRIKES TWICE

"There's this Chinese saying, 'Your strengths become your weakness,'" explains Peter Herz. "You go through this process of really working to build a company, and build the plan, and think through it. And it takes a lot to get a VC to put money into that, so you really clarify your thinking. But if you have a giant exit, then you go back and you have the next idea. You may get that funded more easily because of your prior success—investors may not test your thinking and your plan as thoroughly; maybe you didn't have to go through the thinking and work and clarity of thought to really build the plan right. As a result, quite often, it does seem that the second time around, things don't work out as well. Certainly, part of the explanation is that luck dominates outcomes."

While not overtly endorsing the concept of a "sophomore curse," several interviewees cautioned against financially backing someone who's already had one big success. One of the advisors I interviewed noted that founders and employees may become overconfident about having a second big success: "They might have a false sense that everything they touch turns to gold." He continues: "I know somebody that was a very early person at a video hosting service company. He did well financially and is now working on another startup. My two cents when I hear his idea is I think, 'God what a stupid idea.' You can become delusional that this is the greatest thing, and you throw money at it. Maybe you don't have the perspective to understand that it isn't going to be the best thing. Yet there are certainly people that have been repeat [successful] entrepreneurs."[62]

Along the same lines, Lee Pantuso, a CFO who has been involved with VC firms for decades, explains, "Maybe they're not going to be as diligent this time because they think luck is with them. But [they believe success] really doesn't have anything to do with luck because they're so special."[63] John Bowen notes many who have had $10 million-plus exits "feel the need to take higher risk. I've got a couple friends that walked away with several hundred million, and they took a little time off and then tried to show how smart they were and proceeded to lose a tremendous amount of money, and then closed down the [new] company."

"Check your enthusiasm," is Pantuso's advice. Double-check the thesis with thorough research to determine if the company is on the right path before you invest.

A Serial Success Story & Some Luck

Pouring the proceeds from a liquidity event into another company can put you on the fast track to foreclosure, but the opposite can—and does—happen. Take Peter Thiel, who co-founded PayPal in December 1998 and served as the company's chairman and CEO. In October 2002, eBay acquired PayPal for $1.5 billion, netting Thiel a total of $60 million.[64] Two years later, Thiel made a $500,000 angel investment in a then-small Internet startup called Facebook,[65] and became the company's first outside investor.[66]

A decade after selling PayPal, Thiel experienced his second, much larger, liquidity event, and immediately after Facebook's IPO sold approximately one-third of his 44.7 million Facebook shares for gross proceeds of $633 million.[67] An impressive return on a $500,000 investment!

Regardless of your past successes or failures, confidence, or business plan, luck can ultimately make or break an investment. So while some serial investors continue to succeed, it is important to recognize there is no surefire formula, as Mark Cameron White explains: "I don't care how experienced you are, you cannot tell how a company is going to do when it is first formed. I've had companies that I just thought would not do anything, and they've done spectacularly well. Companies that ought to, on paper, do extremely well, have done nothing."

Peter Herz thoughtfully seconds White: "I know a lot of people that have had giant successes and a lot of people who have failed miserably. There's a subset of people who think success is theirs because they're smart and hardworking, and they don't attribute, either at all or sufficiently, the role of luck in their outcomes." While it may seem tempting to assume you have the golden touch when investing in startups, if you give yourself time to conduct thorough research and commit to participating in the venture before you write a check, you'll increase your chances of success.

Playing in the Wrong Game

Former Facebook president Sean Parker and his Napster co-founder Shawn Fanning deplore the fact that many entrepreneurs move into an angel investment capacity after a success. Seconding this distaste, Marc Andreessen, a Netscape co-founder and now a general partner at the VC firm Andreessen Horowitz, compares an entrepreneur taking on the role of an investor to "Michael Jordan playing baseball."[68] It can be hard to imagine failure after wild success. Yet just as Jordan is not suited to baseball,[69] most baseball players shouldn't switch to technology, as in the case of Curt Schilling (see sidebar). Unfortunately, wild failure is entirely possible after a wild success and can put your employees' livelihoods and your family's future security at risk.

CASE STUDY

GAME OVER: FROM BASEBALL TO BANKRUPTCY

A PITCHER'S PASSION FOR COMPUTER GAMES COSTS HIM $50 MILLION.

Curt Schilling was a superstar baseball player who amassed legions of fans pitching for the Philadelphia Phillies, the Arizona Diamondbacks, and the Boston Red Sox. In 2007, the year he played in his final Major League Baseball game, he earned $13 million.[70]

In addition to his love of baseball, Schilling had a lifelong passion for computer games. Confident and determined, he decided to use part of his $90 million personal fortune to start a computer gaming company and build a massively multiplayer online game (MMO). He started 38 Studios with a $5 million personal investment, and ended up throwing in $50 million of his own money, plus $75 million in Rhode Island taxpayer funds. Near the end of his venture, Schilling had a burn rate of $4 million a month, which he funded from his personal coffers.[71]

The company started by treating its employees very well, yet ended with early cancellation of health insurance and loyal staff going more than a month without pay. A stunned Schilling did not want to admit defeat: "It wasn't that I didn't want to tell anyone," he says. "It's I didn't know what to say."[72]

Because of his fame, the baseball hero was able to get meetings easily as he built the company. One important meeting was with Todd Dagres, an influential, Boston-based venture capitalist specializing in high tech. According to *Boston* magazine, when Dagres's baseball-star glasses came off, he could focus on business—but he didn't like what he saw. Dagres passed on investing in 38 Studios, claiming, "I was a little nervous."[73] Why? Upon questioning, he gave the following reasons:

- Schilling was overconfident. He didn't understand the huge bet he was making with the video gaming company.
- The company would require loads of cash for many years. If the game never made it, investors would lose everything they put in.
- Missing from the 38 Studios team were experienced executives with MMO history.
- Schilling was the owner, not the CEO, yet he acted like he was in control.
- The COO was Schilling's relative.
- Schilling offered too small of a slice of his company to potential investors. (Dagres's usual stake is 20%.)[74]

Not one investor checkbook opened during the six years of the company's existence. Only the State of Rhode Island invested, in the form of a $75 million loan guarantee in return for bringing jobs to the economically distressed state.[75] One of the saddest signs that his company was failing was exhibited during the lunch hour: walking through the office, you would see employees playing competitors' video games.

Problems and Lessons Learned from Curt Schilling's Story

- **Aspiring to be "Bill Gates rich."** Schilling admired Gates's philanthropy and wanted to emulate it by setting up an autism research center (he has an autistic son).[76] Charitable donations come in all sizes, and had he donated a chunk of his original $90 million of earnings from baseball,[77] Schilling could have made a large impact on autism research.

- **Believing you are invincible.** Schilling was a leading player on three different World Series teams. He led the Philadelphia Phillies to the World Series in 1993, won the World Series with the Arizona Diamondbacks in 2001, and took the title again in 2004 and 2007 as a member of the Boston Red Sox.[78] In a *Boston* magazine article, he says of his failed high-tech venture, "I never doubted I was going to do it. My whole life was doing things people didn't believe were possible."[79] The overconfident attitude that made Schilling a leader on the baseball field didn't translate as well into entrepreneurship, where the most successful leaders are visionaries who remain open to the input of others.

- **Thinking that success in one area guarantees future success in another industry.** Schilling suggested that all employees adopt a baseball player–type schedule of working 14 straight days, then taking five days off. The concept of a vacation had to be explained to him.

- **Nepotism is a dirty word if you're looking for investors.** Schilling filled his company with relatives, including his wife on the board of directors, his father-in-law in IT, his mother-in-law as manager of the corporate charity, and his wife's uncle as COO. While the uncle was a seasoned businessman, he had no video game experience. Schilling even referred to him as "Uncle Bill" until he was told by the uncle to stop.[80]

- **Keeping employees from owning the company in the form of stock options.** Schilling was fanatic about keeping control of the company without giving up any ownership to loyal employees, and lost out on early prospective hires who could have helped the company take off in the right direction. He eventually awarded stock options to employees.

- **Not treating your startup like a startup.** The team at 38 Studios worked "too slowly," said Schilling after the fact. He treated employees to gold-star health coverage, large employer-matching on 401(k) contributions, free gym memberships, and new laptops one Christmas. High-level executives enjoyed free lunches and dinners and a big travel budget. These perks are highly unusual for the normally chaotic and cost-conscious Phases 1 and 2 of a startup, and send a message that there is plenty of money. Even Schilling admits to being "comfortable" and having a "sense of invulnerability" during these phases.

- **"Successful pivots are rare,"** writes *Fortune* magazine Senior Editor Dan Primack.[81] "It is extraordinarily difficult for someone at the top of one field to reach the top of another, totally unrelated field. Schilling did try to hire experienced gaming execs to help fill in the blanks, but ultimately he was an ex-ballplayer in charge of a digital content corporation."

Curt Schilling's startup nightmare isn't over yet. According to a February 25, 2013, article on CNN.com, he auctioned and sold the famous "bloody sock" he wore in the 2004 World Series championship for $92,613.[82] In addition, SI.com reported on October 4, 2012, that Schilling was trying to sell a baseball cap worn by New York Yankees great Lou Gehrig and a prized collection of World War II memorabilia. According to SI, these attempts to get revenue are in addition to putting his 20-room, 26-acre Massachusetts home on the market.[83]

Post-Liquidity Plans

For the rare entrepreneur who retires completely or takes a few years off from work, having a plan for your finances and your time will help to keep you happy and your family secure.

A FAILURE TO LAUNCH

One successful Internet portal executive told me about a friend who still has not found his way after involvement in an IPO. This friend, an early Google employee, became financially independent when Google went public but had no plan for his sudden and unexpected wealth.

Now, he and his wife "are just hanging out. He plays video games and plays golf and takes care of the kids," but "that's just kind of it. They're stagnant. Financially they're fine, but they're not really doing anything that gives them purpose," my source explains, sadly. "He's just a failure to launch."

The friend bought a house on the beach in California just because he thought it could be fun to walk the family dogs there. "You've got to find a purpose," the executive stresses. When asked what he'd tell his friend if he were a disinterested party, the executive thoughtfully replied, "You're an Ivy League–educated person. Surely, your time and intellect are worth something. Just find a cause."[84]

BEYOND MONEY: ENJOYING LIFE

After counseling tech titans for more than 20 years in his capacity as a financial advisor, John Bowen has also gone through two liquidity events of his own. He agrees that without at least a rough sketch of a plan beforehand, people can flounder after an event. "I ended up playing with venture capital firms, trying to decide whether I wanted to do consulting or be a CEO in residence," he recalls. "Then, I got asked to be on some boards. I decided it didn't make sense for what I wanted to do, and I started to get focused," he says about the time before he started his large-scale coaching firm. In his time in Silicon Valley, Bowen has seen many entrepreneurs take the following progression: "You either join another team, you start another team, or you go to beefy private equity or on a board where you act as an advisor."

Phase 3 is often not about the money. "The challenge when you have more money is that you have more opportunities," says Bowen. "You also have the ability to ask more questions, and you attract a lot of people for business opportunities [and] charitable giving." As a society, he explains, we are taught that if you work hard, you get enough chips, and then you get off the treadmill—that's the game. Yet, the reality is that it's not that simple.

This is why, Bowen stresses, particularly early on it's so important to have a team of professional advisors you trust and can grow with you. Consulting financial, legal, and business professionals will help you make smart decisions about the next phase of your life, to ensure your wealth is protected and preserved.

WHAT'S NEXT?

If you were born with the entrepreneurial bug, creating companies is the ideal life. You love the innovation and impact of your work, along with the intellectual stimulation of building a company from the ground up. Many entrepreneurs have tried life on the other side—as an employee in an established company—only to conclude they prefer to make a meaningful contribution to society on their own terms. This is especially true after an entrepreneur experiences extreme financial success.

Mitch Anthony, a consultant to the financial services industry calls this the "Encore Retirement," in which "individuals . . . treat their lives as an evolving mission and exploration." For entrepreneurs, it means continually returning to Phase 1 with the flexibility to create companies that align with your values. While for some, a life-changing exit means enjoying a more balanced personal and work life,[85] others—especially younger entrepreneurs—will work just as hard the second time around.

Case in point: one successful entrepreneur made tens of millions after his e-commerce business went public and then started a social networking company that demanded more long, stressful hours. Just after the deal for his last company's acquisition was announced, he had told his executive team, "This is my last startup."[86] In confidence, one of his executive team members confessed doubts, since this serial founder thrives on designing and building products. Besides, he confessed that he has no hobbies.

Another entrepreneur explained, "When I exited my last company, I said I'm never starting another." Yet, she ended up sitting on the board of her son's tech startup, working hard to help him build his dream. "I've ended up way more involved than I thought I was going to [be], and feeling that excitement again of what it's like to just start out fresh, and that for me probably is the most satisfying [thing]."

All of my entrepreneur interviewees went back to a startup after their first (and for a lucky few, second or third) success. Some are taking their time to find the right fit.

FINANCIAL PLANNING AND TAX TIPS

TIP 8   10b5-1 Plans

Many financial and legal folks I interviewed mentioned the benefits of having a 10b5-1 plan in place. These plans are designed for executives—although employees may also use them—to exercise or sell company stock without being subject to insider trading rules or blackout windows. Number of shares to be traded, share price, and dates are the triggers used for trading company stock under a 10b5-1 plan. Most importantly, a plan can be tailored to the specific needs of the individual who sets it up.[87]

A white paper from Silicon Valley law firm Morrison & Foerster explains the rule this way:

> A Rule 10b5-1 plan is a written plan for trading securities that is designed in accordance with Rule 10b5-1(c). Any person executing pre-planned transactions pursuant to a Rule 10b5-1 plan that was established in good faith at a time when that person was unaware of material non-public information has an affirmative defense against accusations of insider trading, even if actual trades made pursuant to the plan are executed at a time when the individual may be aware of material, non-public information that would otherwise subject that person to liability under Section 10(b) of the Exchange Act or Rule 10b5-1. Accordingly, Rule 10b5-1 plans are especially useful for people presumed to have inside information, such as officers and directors.[88]

TIP 9   Alternative Minimum Tax (AMT) Triggers

The alternative minimum tax is a parallel tax system running alongside the regular federal income tax. When your AMT is higher than your regular tax, you'll pay AMT. The top AMT tax rate is 28%.

The most common items that cause individuals to fall into AMT are state taxes, property taxes, and the exercise of incentive stock options (ISOs). State and property taxes are allowed as a deduction from your regular tax but not for AMT, so they effectively increase your AMT tax. When you exercise and hold ISOs, the bargain element—the difference between your option strike price and the fair market value on the date you exercise them—is added to your AMT income.

Tax planning at the end of the year is helpful to analyze your situation and recommend an appropriate plan.

> **If you are not in AMT,** and anticipate a large state tax bill for the year, you'll get a federal tax deduction by paying your state tax by December 31. This planning tool is most useful for people in high-tax states such as California and New York. Alternatively, if you have unexercised ISOs, you can exercise and hold them and pay no tax on the transaction, as long as your AMT doesn't exceed your regular tax. The advantage of exercising and holding ISOs is that you'll get the long-term capital gain holding period started.

> **If you are in the Alternative Minimum Tax (AMT)**, some typical tax deductions will have the opposite effect; they will not decrease your tax liability. If you are in AMT already—for example, perhaps you've paid a large amount of state taxes, claimed many personal exemptions, or have exercised ISOs—you will not want to pre-pay state taxes or property tax. If you expect an additional state tax liability for the current year, make your fourth quarter estimated tax payment in January of the following year.

TIP 10 Cashless Collar

A cashless collar is a technique that combines an individual's large position in the stock of one company with the purchase of a put option and the sale of a call option. The term "collar" relates to both a minimum and maximum value for that position. A fee is paid to guarantee the value of the stock can't go below a certain amount (even though the stock price might). However, your upside potential is also limited. A collar is a conservative strategy, since it preserves the value of an existing stock position from a severe price decline while allowing participation in a portion of any price increase in the stock during the term of the collar.

TIP 11 Charitable Donor-Advised Funds

Donating appreciated securities, instead of cash, to fund charitable bequests is a great tax planning idea if you hold low-cost-basis securities (holdings acquired for much less than their worth today), such as pre-IPO or pre-acquisition stock.

In most cases, you can reduce your taxable income by the amount of gifts made to charity. For example, a donor in the 45% federal and state combined tax bracket would generally receive $4,500 in tax savings from a $10,000 charitable contribution. Such gifts of appreciated stock are deductible at the fair market value (as long as you have held them more than a year), effectively allowing you to avoid paying taxes on the capital gain (appreciation).

Gifts of appreciated securities can be made directly to a qualified charity or to a donor-advised charitable fund. Benefits of a donor-advised fund include ease of funding and transfer, relatively low cost, and avoidance of tax return filing requirements. Your tax deduction is taken in the year of the transfer to the fund, and contributions to individual charities can be made any time in the future.

Once an investment is received by the "sponsoring organization," such as Schwab or a community foundation, the transferred security is liquidated and placed into one or more pooled accounts selected by the donor. The donor can then use these funds to make cash gifts to charitable organizations. The gifts can be made all in one year or over several years.

TIP 12 Dollar Cost Averaging

Dollar cost averaging (DCA) is a strategy used to invest slowly in your portfolio, rather than investing everything at once. A three-, six-, nine-, 12-, or 18-month DCA is usually appropriate when you're investing a large portion of your assets in the market; for example, if you sell your company stock, which was the majority of your net worth, or if you received an inheritance. A DCA is also reasonable if you are concerned about investing at the top of the market (granted, no one has a crystal ball, so no one knows in advance where the top of the market is). If you have a very long time horizon—at least 10 to 15 years—until you need the funds, it's very likely the market will be higher in 10 years than it is today, even if it goes down for some period of time in the interim. The downside to dollar cost averaging is that trading fees are potentially doubled up. Investing the entire amount at once means you pay trading fees only once.

TIP 13 Tax Loss Harvesting

Here is a very simple example of a tax loss harvesting strategy, assuming a combined federal and state tax rate of 40%.

You sell your company for $10 million and after paying taxes, invest the net proceeds of $6 million into a diversified portfolio. The market falls by 20% and you have $4.8 million left. All positions are at a loss, and you sell all $4.8 million of securities in the portfolio, taking a tax loss of $1.2 million. You invest all $4.8 million of sales proceeds into similar securities to retain your asset allocation exposure. Three years later, your portfolio is worth $8.64 million, up by 80% from the low. You have also captured $1.2 million of tax losses that you can use to offset capital gains this year or in future years—from events like selling your company, selling any stock at a gain, or capital gain distributions from your investment portfolio. Note that gain on the sale of restricted stock may only be offset by capital losses to the extent the price of the stock has risen since the vest date.

As long as your portfolio losses come in the year of—or the year(s) before—your liquidity event (the sale of low-priced stock options or your company), your taxes can be lowered. Unfortunately, if the losses happen in a year after the liquidity event, you can't reduce the gain on the sale, but you can reduce current-year or future-year income (from capital gains) by the losses harvested. This strategy only works with a taxable account, not an IRA or 401(k).

TIP 14 Investment Time Horizon

Investing by definition means taking on risk; markets are volatile but over long periods of time produce returns higher than inflation. On the graph below, note the volatility and long-term performance of five asset classes over an 87-year time horizon: U.S. Treasury bills (cash), long-term bonds, corporate bonds, large-cap stocks, and small-cap stocks, looking at historical 25-year holding periods.

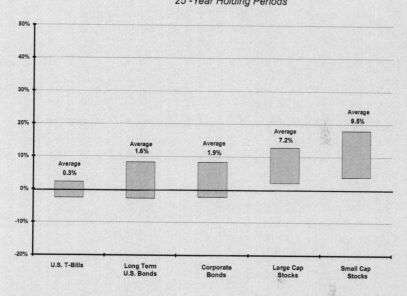

**Inflation Adjusted Returns
1926 - 2013**

25 -Year Holding Periods

Figure 9. Inflation adjusted returns for 25-year holding periods from 1926 to 2013.[89]

In each 25-year holding period, large- and small-cap stocks have never had negative returns. This may seem counterintuitive, but it makes sense: you're paid more to hold riskier assets, and over time, returns converge on long-term historical performance. Therefore, it's important to hold cash in the short term and invest in a diversified equity portfolio for the long term.

A financial planning partner can help you avoid the emotional pitfalls involved in concentration and diversification, adjust investment plans to a comfortable level of risk for you, and have meaningful conversations to better understand what's important to you.

Checklist for Startup Founders in Phase 3

CORPORATE ISSUES

❏ Consider putting a Section 10b5-1 plan in place for the company.

❏ Encourage executives to seek out unbiased financial planning advice.

❏ Continue to work with a corporate attorney as needed.

PERSONAL ISSUES

❏ Diversify, if you are holding a concentrated position in the stock of any one company. Use the Decision Tree Analysis on page 117 to determine the ideal time to sell stock. Consider setting price targets and time triggers on your stock so that it gets sold automatically when a certain price is reached.

❏ Sign up for the 10b5-1 plan to sell your stock on an ongoing basis regardless of blackout windows.

❏ If you haven't done so already, research and hire a financial planner (or spend the time to plan your financial life yourself). Strategize what your assets will accomplish and execute your plan. Be sure to review your risk tolerance (which may have changed since Phase 1). Determine your "Maintain," "Risk," and "Give" Buckets via financial modeling. Your Risk Bucket will determine how much you will invest in your next venture, or use for angel or venture investing.

❏ Create and implement an investment plan. Understand your short- and long-term risk tolerance.

❏ If you're a DIYer, you'll get no value from an unimplemented plan, so be sure to make the time to plow through all your action items and meet any deadlines.

❏ Update or create estate-planning documents incorporating your goals and values. Set up a trust to protect your privacy and other documents to carry out your wishes. Revisit your estate plan if it has been more than five years since you created it.

❏ Consider whether charitable giving is important to you. If so, start to create and execute a charitable giving strategy.

❏ Hold regular family meetings to discuss goals and wealth preservation (or, if you are single, check in with yourself).

❏ As family challenges arise, take advantage of employee assistance programs that your mature or maturing company may provide.

HIRING AN ADVISOR AT ANY PHASE

WHAT IS YOUR HIGHEST AND BEST USE? Former Oracle CFO Roy Bukstein encourages people to explore the best use of their time. Are you comfortable with your level of knowledge and the time you can commit to managing your personal finances? While you're probably "capable of managing it now," he says, situations change over time. People get busy, go through life changes (such as having children or taking on a demanding new job), and the unexpected can happen, too. Is your spouse up to the challenges of managing your finances if you are unable to do so?

"Come to grips with the fact that you can't do it all," stresses Bukstein. If you want a high probability of achieving your goals, hiring an advisor is a smart decision. An objective advisor will keep you grounded in a volatile market and cautious in the face of a stock market that races upward very quickly.

Paying a management fee frees you up to focus on things you enjoy, so you no longer have the burden of monitoring your investments. If you have a personal financial advisor, you should receive ongoing guidance on reducing taxes and personalized advice from a professional who understands your specific situation. The benefit of a financial advisor increases as time goes on. Having someone on call who knows your situation and can answer your questions thoughtfully, with guidance customized to your circumstances, is very valuable.

John Bowen, CEO of CEG Worldwide, believes the fee paid to a financial advisor should translate into "10 times its value received by the client."[1] After spending 26 years as a Silicon Valley financial advisor and helping to manage more than $1.6 billion in assets, Bowen now runs a firm that coaches financial advisors from around the country. He explains the multiplier via email: "The anecdotal experience is that [adding at least 10 times the value of the fees] is not a very high benchmark for top financial advisors to meet when they're delivering a world-class wealth management experience. The combination of improved return on a risk-adjusted basis, lower costs, mitigation of taxes, more effective estate planning, asset protection, and more impactful charitable planning for most clients should be well over 10 times the annual advisory fee."[2]

Benefits of Having a Personal Financial Beacon

Here's a brief—but important—list of the reasons why you should consider outsourcing your personal financial management:

- **It's a time-saver.** Any hour you are not reviewing, researching, implementing, and monitoring your investments and financial plan is time you can devote to work, family, or fun.
- **Access to the most up-to-date news and industry trends.** Your financial planner should be watching out for you and incorporating relevant news into the guidance you receive.
- **Practical knowledge blended with insight tailored to your personal situation.** With an ongoing and intimate relationship, your advisor can give you personalized answers in just a few minutes.
- **It's a one-stop solution.** Most advisors can call on a team of experts to help with the myriad of financial decisions that come up. Ideally, a financial planner should facilitate access to a strong network if outside help is needed.

Financial Planners Versus "Hair and Tooth Guys"

Independent financial planners have a different skill set than representatives from brokerage firms, sometimes known as "financial guys," who buy and sell stocks and bonds but do not have a duty to act in their clients' best interest. The SEC defines the suitability standard for an advisor as "a reasonable basis for believing that the recommendation is suitable for you." But a suitable recommendation is not necessarily the best. Contrast this with the fiduciary standard of care demanded of registered investment advisors (RIAs): "The advisor must place the client's best interest above his own."[3]

A helpful planner is able to dive deeply enough to understand your goals and values, and then establish and strengthen the client-advisor relationship with good communication and empathy—skills that are not taught in business school. Of course, a planner's ability to accurately crunch numbers to arrive at conclusions for the amount of, say, life insurance you need, or the benefit of a doing a Roth IRA conversion, is a given.

In contrast, the average private client guy at a prominent investment bank is often known as a "hair and tooth guy," according to one advisor. These public-facing folks serving individual clients at many large brokerage firms are typically "not super quantitative. A lot of times, frankly, they're just sales guys."[4]

At the end of the day, the hair and tooth guys have to be loyal to their employers; RIAs are more likely to have your best interest at heart.

One entrepreneur/CEO I spoke with has money invested in the private banks of five Wall Street firms.[5] With some surprise he says, "What I learned the hard way is that all these guys might have great names, and you've heard of them before, and maybe over the years they've done well, but I'm very disappointed with the returns that I've had." In the 1990s and early 2000s, when most asset classes were up, he remembers, his bankers "were in the right place at the right time." But in 2007, "the first time there was a hiccup, these guys folded like a cheap suit."

At the private banks, says the entrepreneur/CEO, there's a risk. "They often push whatever is coming down the pike, because they get such a nice commission off of it." Yet, he believes, "These guys in their minds are actually trying very hard to make you money and think they're doing a good job. They have very good backgrounds and MBAs from very prestigious schools in general. So it's not like they're bad guys." However, he cautions that investors should understand the target market of their advisors. If you don't meet the private bank minimum, you'll get an advisor who is "down the food chain," meaning not much experience or skill.

Independently wealthy himself, the entrepreneur/CEO acknowledges that hiring an independent advisor who is paid a percentage of assets to help clients do the right thing is a good idea, especially for someone without trading acumen.

At the Silicon Valley office of Fenwick & West, Darrell Kong knew many entrepreneurs, venture capital investors, and industry executives who had liquidity events. When I asked him how people find a financial planner, he said, "My guess is that there are a lot of financial advisors that are prospecting up and down the Peninsula. They're probably tracking the same news services that I'd use as far as seeing who has become successful, at least as far as raising the bigger rounds. You can project the companies that are doing well and just get in front of them."

If you're contacted by a salesperson to manage your financial life, be sure to ask a lot of questions. You want to make sure you're trusting your money and your life to someone whose skills and interests are in the right place—firmly aligned with your goals. Keep reading for a list of probing questions to ask.

Before You Hire a Financial Planner

Increase your chances of success by taking time to do your research before choosing a financial planner, and be sure to interview at least two candidates before you commit. Understand the fee structure, since any fees are a headwind to your portfolio returns. Below are some great questions to start you off.

- What are your financial planning credentials and designations?
- How long have you been offering financial planning services?
- What is your process for working with clients?
- Will you—or one of your associates—work directly with me on an ongoing basis?
- Do you or your firm receive financial incentives by recommending certain financial products?
- Do you offer ongoing advice regarding my non-investment financial affairs, and look at my entire financial picture?
- Do you and your firm have a fiduciary duty to act in your clients' best interest?
- Can I access my information, account balances, and performance reports on demand?
- How are you and your firm paid? List all sources including asset management fees, trading and insurance commissions, mutual fund expense ratios, sales fees on mutual funds with loads, and revenue sharing with business partners.

Hiring a financial planner is a commitment that should be taken seriously; you should only do it after a significant amount of research. You might also want to consider these issues before you hire:

- Read the firm's website. Does the tone of the communication resonate with you? Do the steps outlined and process described make sense?

- Does the firm do real, analysis-intensive financial planning looking at your assets and annual cash flow projections?

- Will the advisors project what your cash flow and assets look like in the future? Will they project children's educational expenses? Do they show these projections in today's dollars (not future dollars)? And will they provide you with backup for their conclusions?

- Do the advisors prepare an after-tax cash flow projection to determine how much you can add to your portfolio? Or do they take shortcuts and ask you to estimate—or worse, just guess—how much excess cash you have?

- Do they anticipate—and ask about—lifestyle changes as part of your long-term plan, such as additional vacation in retirement or childcare costs if you are about to start a family?

- Do the advisors have a team of experts, such as attorneys and CPAs, available to assist you?

- Are the financial planning and investment management fees reasonable? My firm believes total fees above 1% (on the value of the portfolio of at least $500,000) are too high, and that for portfolios above $2 million, the break-point fee for managing assets above that amount should be less than 1%. This fee should include financial planning, or else it should be lower.

- Do the advisors recommend funds from the universe of mutual funds, or do they favor proprietary funds packaged and sold by their firm? Proprietary funds generally have high fees and are sold to captive clients.

- Does the firm serve people in a similar situation to yours?

- How does the firm report on your performance—by total portfolio, by account, or by holding? The most transparent reporting method is to compare the returns of the total portfolio (all accounts, combined) after fees to a blended benchmark representing your risk profile.

- During your interviews with potential advisors, are their questions designed to learn about your holdings so that they can sell a financial product? Or are they designed to help them understand you, your family, and your comfort with risk?

Additional Advisor Advantages

A knowledgeable and experienced financial planner can add plenty of value. A competent advisor can:

- **Look out for you.** While it's important to look out for yourself, it can be extremely helpful to have a professional double-check your decisions and calculations to make sure you are protected.
- **Reduce your taxes.** Loss harvesting (see page 164) and thoughtful placement of holdings can create a tax-efficient investment portfolio.
- **Serve as your personal CFO.** Your personal financial manager can lead or direct your personal financial affairs and coordinate interaction between various advisors, such as accountants, attorneys, and insurance brokers.
- **Mitigate worry.** A professional advisor can oversee the daily activity of your investments and make changes as soon as they are needed.
- **Help with cash flow planning.** In cash-flush times, an advisor can help you look at cash flow to determine your surplus for the year and, when possible, add the excess to your long-term savings. In lean-cash years, an advisor can formulate a tax-efficient strategy for raising cash or cutting expenses to meet ongoing needs.
- **Keep you invested during jittery markets, and help you reap the rewards of long-term equity returns.** (See "Annualized Investor Returns Versus Benchmarks" on page 131.)
- **Track progress toward your goals.**
- **Protect what you've earned.** Having adequate protection and insurance—for yourself and your property—ensures your assets will not be taken away in a lawsuit.

- **Simplify your life by consolidating multiple accounts.**
- **Help create strategies for passing assets to heirs.**
- **Create a plan to save for your children's college education in a tax-advantageous way.**

What Clients Say About Working with a Professional Financial Planner

Whether delegation comes easily to you, or you are willing to try it for the expectation of a better life, read on to discover the benefits of professional management directly from a handful of interviewees for this book. Names have been changed, and comments have been condensed for clarity.

BOB & CARRIE

Bob and Carrie are a married couple with a 20-year age difference. They enjoy the following aspects of working with a wealth planning firm:

- A deep knowledge of personal finance.
- Patience to answer questions about the markets, performance, and our own situation.
- Personable, with the ability to make things easy to understand, since we are people who have no interest in finance.
- Ongoing education.
- One or two primary advisor contacts who deeply understand our situation.
- Support staff who care about us and are available for general questions.
- Personalized service.
- Annual meetings are very thorough, reviewing all areas of our financial life, which could take two to three hours.
- Written follow-up after meetings, providing a list of recommendations and action items.
- Our advisor has access to the brainpower of other financial professionals through memberships in professional organizations and voluntary study groups.[6]

DAN & ELLIE

Dan, who has worked in tech companies for more than three decades, and his wife, Ellie, are newly retired and enjoy traveling the world. "On our own, we would not have thought about looking out 20 years beyond retirement," Dan says.[7] Dan and Ellie's list of the major benefits of working with a financial planning firm includes:

- The weeding out of extraneous information that's on the web. There are hundreds, if not thousands, of online tools, but which ones can be trusted?
- Comprehensive planning projections right before we stopped working gave us answers about whether we had enough to maintain our lifestyle.
- We like being challenged about what we want to achieve with our money, and we like being coached about our investment risk level. Our financial planner looks at the big picture and oversees each financial decision.

BRIAN

Brian is a sharp, driven, successful financial executive who could manage his portfolio himself—if it were not so time-intensive. He works long hours and spends his free time snowboarding and hiking. "I want my advisor to look out for opportunities, minimize capital gains and taxes, and create a strategy for me," he says.[8]

He lists these perks of working with an advisor:

- Assists in diversification of company stock; if needed, there is a dialogue and debate about stock option diversification.
- The ability to invest, and stay invested, especially in a difficult market.
- A resource who understands my goals; little background or explanation is needed when I have ongoing questions.
- Direct and thoughtful advice and analysis presented clearly, without a marketing spin.
- Strategic and systematic rebalancing of my portfolio.

You will experience ups and downs in your portfolio, but a long-term financial plan will give you confidence about your future.

Be Sure You're Getting Financial Planning Advice: Regulation of the Financial Services Industry

We rely on the government to protect our food and water supply. Unfortunately, at this time we can't rely on the government to completely oversee the financial industry.

"Financial advisor" and "financial planner" are titles used loosely. The U.S. government does not regulate the use of either. Instead, financial services professionals are regulated by the services they provide. For example, a planner who also provides securities advice is regulated as a stockbroker or investment advisor. As a result, the term "financial planner" may be used in a way that is confusing to consumers.

However, credentials from regulatory agencies and professional associations can be relied upon to explain experience and knowledge. Professional designations are awarded to individuals after intensive training and testing, eliminating potential consumer confusion. Here are definitions of some popular designations:

- **CFP®—CERTIFIED FINANCIAL PLANNER™**. Individuals must have a college degree, work 6,000 hours under strict experience guidelines or 4,000 hours as an apprentice,[9] pass certification classes, and pass a rigorous two-day board exam.
- **CFA—Chartered Financial Analyst.** This credential is focused primarily on investments. CFA Charterholders, as they are called, must have four years of investment work experience and complete three six-hour exams. The CFA is a credential that indicates a depth of investment expertise as well as a vigorous code of ethics and fiduciary duty.
- **CPA—Certified Public Accountant.** Individuals must pass a rigorous exam focused on taxes, accounting, auditing, and business law. Additionally, education and work experience requirements vary by state.
- **CLU—The Chartered Life Underwriter** designation is held by life insurance salespeople.
- **ChFC—A Chartered Financial Consultant** credential requires classes but no comprehensive board exam.[10]

Education, credentials, and experience do matter. Often people in the investment advisory business were trained in another discipline before entering the field. Choose someone who has a technical background such as accounting, engineering, or finance, and say no to working with a former car salesperson or real estate broker.

FEE-ONLY ADVISORS

Fee-only advisors are compensated by clients only, and not from mutual fund or insurance commissions, referral fees, or kickbacks from vendors. Receiving compensation based solely on assets under management or on an hourly basis means the advisor has your best interests in mind and is free of bias toward or against any particular investment or insurance product. The opposite of fee-only is "fee based," meaning that commissions are accepted.

Resources for Finding the Best Advisor for You

What's the best way to choose an advisor?

In addition to asking for recommendations from trusted friends, colleagues, and family, search for planners where they are: on the websites of their professional associations. Be sure to understand each advisor's specialty or niche area. A CERTIFIED FINANCIAL PLANNER™ professional is the gold standard in the professional financial advisor world. Earning the CFP® certification means the advisor has joined a select group of competent and ethical personal financial planning advisors.

THE CERTIFIED FINANCIAL PLANNER BOARD OF STANDARDS (CFP.net)

A CFP® practitioner is required to act in your best interest. Only those who have fulfilled the certification and renewal requirements of the CFP Board can display the CFP® certification trademarks, which represent a high level of competency, ethics, and professionalism. Read more about the CFP® certification and the importance of the designation on this website.

THE FINANCIAL PLANNING ASSOCIATION (FPAnet.org)

Find a financial planner using the resources on this site. The Financial Planning Association® (FPA®) is a membership organization for CFP® professionals in the United States. Members adhere to the highest standards of professional competence, ethical conduct, and clear, complete disclosure to those they serve.

THE NATIONAL ASSOCIATION OF PERSONAL FINANCIAL ADVISORS (NAPFA.org)

This is a membership organization of fee-only financial advisors. Each member must take a fiduciary oath to act in the good faith and in the best interests of the client, and does not receive any compensation that is contingent on any client's purchase or sale of a financial product.[11]

THE GARRETT PLANNING NETWORK (GarrettPlanningNetwork.com)

The Garrett Planning Network has an hourly-based model. Check out the financial planners in the network for a once-a-year review or ongoing assistance.

FINANCIAL PLANNING AND TAX TIPS

TIP 15   **The Best Way to Find an Honest Advisor**

Below, I provide a few ways to help ensure that you are dealing with an advisor who is above board. Honest advisors will gladly comply with these standards and answer your questions. Those with something to hide may deviate from these practices or claim their investment process is "propri- etary" or "too technical" to concern yourself with, as financial con man Bernie Madoff claimed to inquisitive prospective clients.

- Make sure you have access to your account through the custodi- an's website. Custodians are firms like Charles Schwab (and the advisory arm, Schwab Institutional), Fidelity, and TDAmeritrade. It's great if you can see your account balance and performance reports through your advisor's site, too, but make sure you can review your holdings online via a third-party custodian. This way, you can be sure you own what the advisor's statement says.

- The custodian of your assets should have financial statements audited by a U.S.-based auditor. The custodian's financial state- ments should not be just "reviewed" or "compiled," as these are lower standards than a full audit.

- Ask questions about where and why assets are custodied at cer- tain firms. Assets should never be held at the advisor's firm (unless the firm also operates as a custodian), and never with the same party who directs the accounts.

- Confirm that monthly or quarterly statements will be delivered online or by mail from a third-party custodian, not the money manager.

- Understand how your assets are safeguarded, and who the advi- sor shares information with other than you. Information is often shared through paper or electronic reports, or via web access through the advisor's client portal in addition to the custodian's website.

- The potential advisor (or someone at the firm) should patiently respond to any and all questions about investment philosophy, asset allocation, and risk. Educational questions are an important way to gauge comfort with an advisor. (See "Before You Hire a Financial Planner" beginning on page 171 for a list of questions.)

- The advisor should be able to provide backup for the work performed on your behalf, such as detailed year-by-year cash flow projections when preparing a retirement or life insurance analysis, and the formula used to calculate your investment performance.
- Ideally, the advisor will clearly state fees on performance reports. Performance should be shown net of fees, unless otherwise stated.
- Your accounts should be in your own name and not commingled with the assets of other clients or in the name of the firm.
- Ask for references from existing long-term clients in a similar life or career situation to you (for example, high-tech executives with stock-option planning issues or divorced women). Contact at least two longtime clients to ask about ongoing access and services.
- You should feel comfortable talking with the advisor. Your advisor should understand your goals and values, and talking to that person should be a pleasant and not at all concerning experience.
- If the advisor uses mutual funds, exchange traded funds (ETFs), and/or publicly traded stocks and trades through a known outside custodian, this would indicate a low risk of shifty behavior—that is, a high chance your assets are safe from pilfering or Ponzi schemes. However, the skills of stock picking and/or asset allocation still must be assessed.

At the end of the day, hiring an advisor is a leap of faith. However, doing your due diligence and using the information presented in this section should give you a very high degree of confidence about moving forward.

CONCLUSION

ENTREPRENEURS ARE PASSIONATE ABOUT creating companies that solve problems. Phases 1 and 2 are the most fun, and Phase 3 is all about getting back to Phase 1 to begin another exciting venture.

Throughout the Entrepreneur's Wheel of Life, the key to a secure financial future is to plan carefully. Whether you choose to go at financial planning alone or outsource to an experienced professional, making and keeping your personal wealth are ongoing enterprises best approached with diligence and foresight.

If you'd like to learn more about the psychological aspects of life before, during, and after a liquidity event, read my white paper "The BE WISE Planning Strategy: A Formula for Financial Success and Personal Happiness." It explores such topics as how to use your resources to create a satisfying life, how much money you should allocate to long-term needs, and how much you can risk on your next company or angel investments. Contemplating these issues regardless of where you are in the Entrepreneur's Wheel of Life can help you identify your passions and strategize your finances accordingly. Download the white paper at JLFwealth.com.

For non-entrepreneurs working in high-tech, my book *Life, Liquidity & the Pursuit of Happiness* explores many of the same themes as this volume, but with a focus on the experiences of executives and employees, who are more likely to retire—or at least stop working on a daily basis—after a liquidity event than entrepreneurs.

As I've discussed in this book—and you no doubt know from experience—entrepreneurs have distinct concerns and responsibilities and must take action before and after any wealth event to ensure a successful outcome.

Checklist for Startup Founders

Here are the key takeaways.

BEFORE THE EVENT

❏ Plan ahead for taxes. Before you sign a contract, strategize how to spread the income over several years, if it lowers your tax bill.

❏ Consider an all-cash deal. Or, if you decide to sell your company in exchange for stock, recognize that you could be taking a big risk holding stock in a company you don't control.

❏ Don't spend until cash is in the bank. Brace yourself for last-minute business negotiations or the possibility that the acquirer will back out or the IPO will be postponed.

❏ Early exercise your options via a Section 83(b) election. This is often a good idea when the strike price is low.

❏ Do your research. When it comes to attorneys, investment bankers, and other advisors, do your due diligence. You want to make sure that the people giving you advice have your best interest in mind, high ethical standards, and an approach and personality that jibe with yours.

AFTER THE EVENT

❏ Realize that your financial needs have changed. Don't default to using the broker who took your company through its IPO as your personal financial advisor. Do some research. Your personal financial needs are likely not the same as those of your company, and you are under no obligation to stick with your IPO advisor. The most important thing is to make sure the professionals advising you are a good fit to help you achieve your goals.

❏ Sell your company stock to diversify. Sell at least 50% as soon as you can, with a near-term goal of getting down to no more than 5% to 10% of your net worth in company stock. I interviewed dozens of people for this book of varying ages and backgrounds, and nearly every entrepreneur who had gone through a liquidity event repeated some version of the "sell half" rule. A few of my sources even said that they sold 80% or all of their company stock right away.

❑ Earnout goals can jeopardize your wealth. Having to hit a price or revenue target to get cash out of the acquiring company means that you are risking real wealth.

❑ Keep an eye out for fraud. Fraud can happen after a liquidity event when the founder is no longer in control of the company, according to my research.

❑ Protect yourself with a cashless collar. If you are contractually restricted from selling stock, a cashless collar or other structured product can be a great tool for locking in your sales proceeds.

❑ Set up a 10b5-1 plan. This tool enables you to sell stock without being subject to blackout periods or insider training restrictions.

❑ Separate your risk capital from your lifestyle funds. Want to angel invest? Don't risk the funds in your Maintain Bucket. Only use funds in your Risk Bucket.

❑ Plan for life post-liquidity. Recognize that most people leave a company within two years of a liquidity event. Have a plan for how you'll spend your days. Explore your passions. Live your dreams.

True entrepreneurs never retire. You may take a break, but it's likely you'll return to the action in some form, regardless of your wealth, life stage, or lifestyle. Whatever the future holds, you now have the knowledge you need to move proactively and confidently toward the life you want. I wish you the best of luck in your current startup—and whatever's next.

The Entrepreneur's Wheel of Life℠

Pre-Transition Phase
2–40 years

1 Laying the Foundation

Challenges

QUALITY OF LIFE
- Preoccupation with startup
- Optimism
- Loneliness
- Improvisation
- Tenacity

FINANCIAL
- Raising capital
- Below-market salary
- Accountability to investors
- Funneling all resources into the company

Most entrepreneurs never retire.

They just keep going back to Phase 1.

Post-Transition Phase
1–24 months

3 Realizing the Dream

Challenges

QUALITY OF LIFE
- Figuring out what's next
- Determining how to return to Phase 1

FINANCIAL
- Accountability to shareholders, board, and management
- Increasing enterprise value
- Strategizing goals with financial resources
- Expensive purchases (home, car, jewelry, boat)

Pre-Transition Phase
0–24 months

2 Ramping Up

Challenges

QUALITY OF LIFE
- Maintaining balance while working long hours
- Excitement
- Persistence

FINANCIAL
- Negotiations
- Increasing enterprise value
- Compensation
- Learning new business skills
- Financial and tax planning
- Accountability to investors and board

LIQUIDITY EVENT

COMMON TO ALL PHASES

Challenge

Maximize Value of Equity Awards (ISO, NQ, RSA, RSU, ESPP)

Concerns

Wealth Preservation
Tax Reduction
Wealth Protection
Passing Assets to Heirs
Charitable Giving

Solutions

Financial Education
Expert Team of Advisors
Personal CFO

ACKNOWLEDGMENTS

This book's unique appeal derives from the generosity of those who shared their experiences working in a startup or advising those who do.

I'd like to thank those who sat for interviews and shared their wisdom and perspectives. They include Sam Adler, John Bowen, Dave Buchanan, Roy Bukstein, Lise Buyer, Ed Callan, Jonathan Cardella, Robert Carter, Mitch Cohen, Stephanie Coutu, Ed Deibert, Lara Druyan, Martin Eberhard, Leland Fong, Eliot Franklin, Mark Galant, Rachel Garb, Eric Gold, Ken Goldman, Jason Graham, Peter Herz, Michael Irvine, Darrell Kong, Jim Koshland, Danny Krebs, Jamis MacNiven, Dee Anna McPherson, Lesa Mitchell, Marlee Myers, Rob Nail, Lee Pantuso, Sonja Hoel Perkins, Richard Pivnicka, Joe Preis, Brendan Richardson, Laura Roden, Stephen Roth, Jeff Russakow, Alexandra Derby Salkin, Santosh Sharan, Tiffany Shlain, David Spark, David Stern, Marc Tarpenning, Nicolai Wadstrom, Rebecca Watson, Bill Weihl, Mark Cameron White, Bruce Wilford, Sylvia Yam, and others who spoke to me on background.

In addition, some interviews were conducted in confidentiality, and the names of those interviewees are withheld by mutual agreement.

I'd also like to thank the following:

My longtime editor, Karen Sulkis, who is a master of turning technical financial subjects into lively, pithy, accessible prose. Karen always meets deadlines and is a great friend.

Tarren Schaar, who I've had the pleasure of working with since 2008, plays a crucial role in our firm on a daily basis. Tarren has been dedicated to serving our clients and making the back office run smoothly. He also read and provided feedback on draft chapters of this book.

Intern Nicole Bauthier helped to streamline a 500-page manuscript into two focused books. She did so with bubbly enthusiasm and a strategic understanding of how books should flow. Rachel Davidson provided further editorial guidance and assistance.

The hundreds of clients I have served over two decades, for their trust and confidence. My clients have allowed me to make a positive impact on their lives by guiding them toward their goals and dreams.

My financial planner colleagues. I'm fortunate to work in a helping profession in which sharing with other advisors benefits the community at large. The following individuals, most of whom are CERTIFIED FINANCIAL PLANNER™ professionals, read drafts of white papers and chapters and provided invaluable feedback: Sandra Bragar, Ketan Desai, Colin Drake, Robert Gavrich, David Gilbert, Emilie Goldman, Janet Hoffmann, Gretchen Hollstein, Heather Hutchinson, Bob Lee, Eric Leve, Brian Pon, and Greg Schick.

An extra-special thank-you to Tim Kochis. Tim, a luminary in the financial planning profession and an accomplished and well-respected author himself, provided feedback on the book outline and my first white paper containing preliminary research for the books.

The Kauffman Foundation, for sponsoring research to help entrepreneurs and startups succeed, and for granting me permission to use some of their findings and graphics in my books.

Samuel Roth, for sharing his decades of business wisdom, and Vanessa Bertini, for her creative inspiration.

Joe Preis and Mark Galant for book title ideas, and Peter Herz for introducing me to the decision tree concept.

Nola Miller for several important introductions.

My book publication team of Holly Brady, Vicky Vaughn Shea, Glenn Randle, Carrie Wicks, and Terry Franklin.

Thank you to Random House President Gina Centrello, who read an early draft of my manuscript and offered invaluable guidance.

Additionally, the following legal, tax, and business professionals provided feedback on the technical sections of the book: John Advani, Paul Allen, Sam Berde, Frank Kearney, Beth Kramer, and Nancy Peck.

Finally, to my husband, Stephen Roth, for allowing me to share the story of his successful liquidity event and the wise planning we did, and for supporting my multiyear dedication to researching and writing these books.

SOURCES

One-Month U.S. Treasury Bills: Total returns in USD. January 1926–Present: One-Month U.S. Treasury Bills. Source: Morningstar. Former Source: Stocks, Bonds, Bills, and Inflation, Chicago: Ibbotson and Sinquefield, 1986.

Long-Term Government Bonds: Total returns net of all fees in USD. January 1926–Present: Long-Term Government Bonds. Source: Morningstar. Former Source: Stock, Bonds, Bills, and Inflation, Chicago: Ibbotson and Sinquefield, 1986.

Long-Term Corporate Bonds: Total returns net of all fees in USD. January 1926–Present: Long-Term Corporate Bonds. Source: Morningstar. Former Source: Stocks, Bonds, Bills, and Inflation, Chicago: Ibbotson and Sinquefield, 1986.

Large-Cap Stocks (S&P 500 Index): Total returns in USD. January 1990–Present: S&P 500 Index.

The S&P Data are provided by Standard & Poor's Index Services Group. January 1926–December 1989: S&P 500 Index. Ibbotson data courtesy of © Stocks, Bonds, Bills and Inflation Yearbook™, Ibbotson Associates, Chicago (annually updated works by Roger C. Ibbotson and Rex A. Sinquefield).

Small-Cap Stocks (CRSP 9-10 Index): CRSP, total returns in USD$. Small Company Universe Returns (Deciles 9 & 10)—All Exchanges. Oct 1988–Present : CRSP Deciles 9-10 Cap-Based Portfolio. Jan 1973–Sep 1988: CRSP Database (NYSE & AMEX & OTC), Rebalanced Quarterly. Jul 1962–Dec 1972: CRSP Database (NYSE & AMEX), Rebalanced Quarterly. Jan 1926–Jun 1962: NYSE, Rebalanced Semi-Annually.

ENDNOTES

Introduction

1. Brendan Richardson, in discussion with the author, April 2012.

2. "Thomas Jefferson," *Wikipedia*, accessed August 11, 2012, http://en.wikipedia.org/wiki/Thomas_Jefferson.

3. Jamis MacNiven, in discussion with the author, January and July 2012.

4. John Brownlee, "Nose Jobs: The Story Behind the Most Incredible Steve Jobs Photo You've Never Seen," Cult of Mac, last updated January 26, 2013, accessed February 2, 2013, http://www.cultofmac.com/212065/nose-jobs-the-story-behind-the-most-incredible-steve-jobs-photo-youve-never-seen-feature/.

5. Jamis MacNiven, email message to author, November 26, 2013.

6. Jamis MacNiven, *Breakfast at Buck's: Tales from the Pancake Guy* (Woodside, CA: Buck's Books, 2004), 6.

7. Robert Metcalfe Inventor Profile, National Inventors Hall of Fame, accessed January 11, 2014, http://invent.org/inductee-detail/?IID=353.

8. Jessica Livingston, *Founders at Work: Stories of Startups' Early Days* (New York, NY: Apress, 2008), 4–5.

9. "History–PayPal," PayPal, accessed February 6, 2013, https://www.paypal-media.com/history.

10. Jamis MacNiven, email to the author, November 26, 2013.

11. Brownlee, "Nose Jobs: The Story Behind the Most Incredible Steve Jobs Photo You've Never Seen."

12. Jamis MacNiven, "The Farm of the Future–An Apology to Steve Jobs–and a RIF on Book Collecting," *Buck's Stories*, last updated December 10, 2011, accessed February 4, 2013, http://bucksstories.blogspot.com/2011/12/farm-of-future-apology-to-steve-jobs.html.

Phase 1: Laying the Foundation

1. "Jonathan Cardella CrunchBase Profile," Crunchbase.com, last updated September 6, 2013, accessed November 2, 2013, http://www.crunchbase.com/person/jonathan-cardella.

2. Jonathan Cardella, LinkedIn profile page, accessed November 2, 2013, http://www.linkedin.com/in/jonathancardella.

3. Jonathan Cardella, in discussion with the author, October 2012.

4. Scale is a term to define growth with operating leverage: as the company's sales rise, the costs of sales, marketing, administration, and research and development do not grow as fast.

5. Strategics are competitors or other companies who acquire an entity or the assets of an entity to plug into their platform, to acquire a team, the intellectual property, or existing market share.

6. Jonathan Cardella, email message to author, December 4, 2013.

7. Mark Cameron White, in discussion with the author, April 2012.

8. Bruce Wilford, in discussion with the author, May 2012.

9. Vivek Wadhwa et al., *The Anatomy of an Entrepreneur: Making of a Successful Entrepreneur* (Kauffman Foundation for Entrepreneurship, November 2009).

10. Ibid.

11. Dave Buchanan, in discussion with the author, August 2012.

12. Mark Galant, in discussion with the author, September 2012.

13. Roy Bukstein, in discussion with the author, December 2011.

14. "Entrepreneur Elon Musk: Why It's Important to Pinch Pennies on the Road to Riches," Knowledge@Wharton, last updated May 27, 2009, accessed September 25, 2012, http://knowledge.wharton.upenn.edu/article.cfm?articleid=2245.

15. Leland Fong, in discussion with the author, February 2012.

16. Chris O'Brien, "How I Made It: Evernote CEO Phil Libin," *L.A. Times*, last updated August 2, 2013, accessed November 2, 2013, http://articles.latimes.com/2013/aug/02/business/la-fi-himi-libin-20130804.

17. "Phil Libin: Vator Splash Keynote Speech, TechTalks.tv video, from a speech given in San Francisco on February 13, 2013, http://techtalks.tv/talks/keynote-presentation-by-phil-libin/57943/.

18. Boonsri Dickinson, "INTERVIEW: Evernote Cofounder Phil Libin Wants To Build A 100 Year Company," *Business Insider*, last updated April 18, 2012, accessed February 14, 2013, http://articles.businessinsider.com/2012-04-18/tech/31359960_1_phil-libin-evernote-bigger-office#ixzz2KtSat56W.

19. Jason Snell, "Steve Jobs: Making a dent in the universe," *Macworld*, last updated October 6, 2011, accessed February 14, 2013, http://www.macworld.com/article/1162827/steve_jobs_making_a_dent_in_the_universe.html.

20. Stephanie Coutu, in discussion with the author, October 2012.

21. Stephanie Coutu, email message to author, December 17, 2013.

22. Michael Irvine, in discussion with the author, August 2012.

23. Interview with engineer and entrepreneur, 2012. Name withheld by mutual agreement.

24. Interview with attorney and high-tech executive, 2012. Name withheld by mutual agreement.

25. Irvine, interview.

26. Interview with attorney and high-tech executive, 2012. Name withheld by mutual agreement.

27. "Constructive dismissal," *Wikipedia*, accessed November 29, 2012, http://en.wikipedia.org/wiki/Constructive_dismissal.

28. Interview with attorney and high-tech executive, 2012. Name withheld by mutual agreement.

29. Danny Krebs, email message to author, December 2, 2013.

30. Danny Krebs, in discussion with the author, January 2013.

31. Interview with engineer and entrepreneur, 2012. Name withheld by mutual agreement.

32. David Stern, in discussion with the author, December 2011.

33. Wadhwa et al., *The Anatomy of an Entrepreneur: Making of a Successful Entrepreneur.*

34. Ibid.

35. "3ware," *Wikipedia*, accessed September 15, 2012, http://en.wikipedia.org/wiki/3ware.

36. Peter Herz, in discussion with the author, July and August 2012.

37. Peter Herz, LinkedIn profile page, accessed March 24, 2013, http://www.linkedin.com/in/jpeterherz.

38. Peter Herz, email message to author, December 3, 2013.

39. Martin Eberhard, in discussion with the author, February 2012.

40. Sylvia Yam, in discussion with the author, July 2012. Although permission was granted to utilize her quotes from 2012, she later expressed via email on January 2, 2014, that recent professional experiences have altered her current opinions on these matters.

41. Sonja Hoel Perkins, in discussion with the author, April 2012.

42. Amy Feldman, "Putting Founders First," *Inc.*, last updated March 1, 2007, accessed November 24, 2012, http://www.inc.com/magazine/20070301/finance-raising-funds.html.

43. Feldman, "Putting Founders First."

44. Scott Edward Walker, "Ask the attorney: How founder friendly is FF stock?," VentureBeat, last updated April 12, 2010, accessed November 24, 2012, http://venturebeat.com/2010/04/12/ask-the-attorney-how-founder-friendly-is-ff-stock/.

45. Sarah Reed and Peter Fusco, "To Buy or Not to Buy? Giving Founders Early Liquidity," *Venture Capital Review* (National Venture Capital Association and Ernst & Young LLP, Winter 2009).

46. Ibid.

47. Walker, "Ask the attorney: How founder friendly is FF stock?"

48. Lara Druyan, in discussion with the author, October 2012.

49. Buchanan, interview.

50. Galant, interview.

51. Buchanan, interview.

52. Ibid.

53. Marc Tarpenning, in discussion with the author, February 2012.

54. Deborah Gage, "The Venture Capital Secret: 3 Out of 4 Startups Fail," *Wall Street Journal*, last updated September 20, 2012, accessed September 20, 2012, http://online.wsj.com/news/articles/SB10000872396390443720204578004980476429190.

55. Ibid.

56. Richard Pivnicka, in discussion with the author, January 2012.

57. Buchanan, interview.

58. Wadhwa et al., "The Anatomy of an Entrepreneur: Making of a Successful Entrepreneur."

59. Kaye A. Thomas, *Consider Your Options: Get the Most from Your Equity Compensation* (Lisle: Fairmark Press, 2000), 168–169.

60. John Pletz, "Good news-bad news scenarios for Groupon shares," *Crain's Chicago Business*, last updated June 1, 2012, accessed November 2, 2013, http://www.chicagobusiness.com/article/20120601/NEWS08/120539949/good-news-bad-news-scenarios-for-groupon-shares#.

61. Aaron Pressman, "Candy Crush Saga Could Be Far Better IPO Story Than Zynga," *Yahoo! Finance*, last updated September 27, 2013, accessed November 2, 2013, http://finance.yahoo.com/blogs/the-exchange/candy-crush-saga-could-far-better-ipo-story-190037091.html.

62. "Taxable and Nontaxable Income," Publication 525, Department of the Treasury, Internal Revenue Service, accessed August 7, 2012, http://www.irs.gov/pub/irs-pdf/p525.pdf.

63. Thomas, *Consider Your Options: Get the Most from Your Equity Compensation*, 56.

64. Ken Goldman, in discussion with the author, March 2012.

65. Jason Graham, email message to author, December 17, 2013.

66. Graham, email message to author, December 27, 2013.

67. "Publication 525 (2013), Taxable and Nontaxable Income," International Revenue Service, accessed January 26, 2013, http://www.irs.gov/publications/p525/ar02.html#en_US_2011_publink1000229243.

68. National Association of Tax Professionals, email message to author, January 9, 2013.

Phase 2: Ramping Up

1. Lesa Mitchell, in discussion with the author, October 2012.

2. Perkins, interview.

3. Interview with engineer and entrepreneur, 2012. Name withheld by mutual agreement.

4. Mitch Cohen, in discussion with the author, October 2012.

5. Loren Feldman, "Goldman Sachs and the $580 Million Black Hole," *New York Times*, last updated July 14, 2012, accessed July 26, 2012, http://www.nytimes.com/2012/07/15/business/goldman-sachs-and-a-sale-gone-horribly-awry.html?pagewanted=all&_r=0.

6. Ibid.

7. Ibid.

8. Ibid.

9. Ibid.

10. Marlee Myers, in discussion with the author, July 2012.

11. Marlee Myers, email message to author, December 20, 2013.

12. Marlee Myers, email message to author, December 13, 2013.

13. Marlee Myers, email message to author, December 20, 2013.

14. Rob Nail, in discussion with the author, July 2012.

15. Marlee Myers, email message to author, December 20, 2013.

16. Santosh Sharan, in discussion with the author, September 2012.

17. Carrie Kirby, "Inside look at a billionaire's budget / Larry Ellison's spending worries his accountant," *San Francisco Chronicle*, last updated January 31, 2006, accessed July 15, 2013, http://www.sfgate.com/news/article/Inside-look-at-a-billionaire-s-budget-Larry-2542603.php.

18. Timothy L. O'Brien, "Fortune's Fools: Why the Rich Go Broke," *New York Times*, last updated September 17, 2006, accessed July 15, 2013, http://www.nytimes.com/2006/09/17/business/yourmoney/17broke.html?pagewanted=all&_r=0.

19. O'Brien, "Fortune's Fools: Why the Rich Go Broke."

20. Ibid.

21. Kirby, "Inside look at a billionaire's budget / Larry Ellison's spending worries his accountant."

22. Ibid.

23. Druyan, interview.

Liquidity Event: The Payoff

1. John Bowen, in discussion with the author, February 2012.

2. Druyan, interview.

3. "Borg (*Star Trek*)," *Wikipedia*, accessed November 6, 2012, http://en.wikipedia.org/wiki/Borg_%28Star_Trek%29.

4. Interview with engineer and entrepreneur, 2012. Name withheld by mutual agreement.

Phase 3: Realizing the Dream

1. "GAIN Capital Group Named to 'Top Ten' on 2005 Deloitte Technology Fast 500," GainCapital.com, last updated October 19, 2005, accessed November 23, 2012, http://ir.gaincapital.com/phoenix.zhtml?c=241648&p=irol-newsArticle&ID=1505375&highlight=.

2. Mark Galant, email message to author, December 16, 2013.

3. "Adventures in New Ventures," Commerce UVa: McIntire School of Commerce at the University of Virginia (Summer 2012).

4. Ibid.

5. Ibid.

6. Interview with entrepreneur and executive, 2012. Name withheld by mutual agreement.

7. Interview with business development executive, 2012. Name withheld by mutual agreement.

8. May 2013.

9. Scott Thurm, "Schmidt to Sell Google Stake Worth $2.5 Billion," *Wall Street Journal*, last updated February 8, 2013, accessed February 9, 2013, http://online.wsj.com/article/SB10001424127887324590904578292541060345994.html?mod=WSJ_article_comments#articleTabs%3Darticle.

10. "Autodesk—Company," accessed November 1, 2012, http://www.autodesk.com/company.

11. Based on the performance of the Russell 3000 Index through December 31, 2013.

12. Joe Preis, in discussion with the author, July 2013.

13. Interview with business development executive, 2012. Name withheld by mutual agreement.

14. Ibid.

15. Wilford, interview.

16. Based on responses from 35 interviewees.

17. Jim Koshland, in discussion with the author, August 2012.

18. Interview with entrepreneur and executive, 2012. Name withheld by mutual agreement.

19. Goldman, interview.

20. Interview with attorney and high-tech executive, 2012. Name withheld by mutual agreement.

21. Bob Gavrich, email message to author, June 12, 2012.

22. The decision tree graphic was made using an Excel add-in made by TreePlan Software (http://www
    .treeplan.com). For more information, see http://www.treeplan.com/treeplan-for-decision-trees.htm.

23. Interview with engineer and entrepreneur, 2012. Name withheld by mutual agreement.

24. Interview with high-tech executive, 2012. Name withheld by mutual agreement.

25. Certified Financial Planner Board of Standards, Inc., "What You Should Know About Financial
    Planning" (CFP Board, 2009).

26. Excerpted from the book *The Investment Answer: Learn to Manage Your Money & Protect Your Financial
    Future* by Daniel C. Goldie, CFA, CFP® and Gordon S. Murray. Copyright © 2011 by Daniel C.
    Goldie and Gordon S. Murray. Reprinted by permission of Business Plus. All rights reserved.

27. James Picerno, "Weights and Bands," *Wealth Manager* (2007), accessed October 25, 2012.

28. New research from Morningstar shows that compared to a DIY investor, the added value of financial
    planning can be an extra 1.82% per year to investment returns. See Returns of DIY Investors section
    beginning on page 130.

29. Interview with business development executive, 2012. Name withheld by mutual agreement.

30. Interview with high-tech executive, 2012. Name withheld by mutual agreement.

31. Roccy DeFrancesco, "2012 DALBAR Study Reveals Average Investor Returns," *Physician's Money
    Digest*, last updated April 20, 2012, accessed September 29, 2012, http://www.physiciansmoney
    digest.com/personal-finance/2012-DALBAR-Study.

32. DALBAR 2012 Quantitative Analysis of Investor Behavior (QAIB) study.

33. Returns data from the DALBAR 2012 Quantitative Analysis of Investor Behavior (QAIB) study.

34. Chuck Jaffe, "Are financial advisers worth their fee?," MarketWatch, last updated September
    26, 2012, accessed October 23, 2012, http://www.marketwatch.com/story/are-financial-advisers-
    worth-their-fee-2012-09-26.

35. Jeff Russakow, in discussion with the author, March 2012.

36. Interview with entrepreneur and executive, 2012. Name withheld by mutual agreement.

37. Linda Himelstein, "Halsey Minor's Major Plans for CNET," Bloomberg *Businessweek*, last updated
    July 26, 1999, accessed August 5, 2013, http://www.businessweek.com/1999/99_30/b3639039.htm.

38. Dawn McCarty and Ari Levy, "How Halsey Minor Blew Tech Fortune on Way to Bankruptcy,"
    Bloomberg, last updated May 31, 2013, accessed August 3, 2013, http://www.bloomberg.com/
    news/2013-05-30/cnet-founder-minor-files-for-bankruptcy-after-selling-art.html.

39. Jessi Hempel, "Web pioneers are back, but not together," CNN Money, last updated August 15, 2008, accessed August 3, 2013, http://money.cnn.com/2008/08/11/technology/cnet_minor_bonnie .fortune/.

40. Dawn McCarty, "Halsey Minor Tries Again for Bankruptcy After Missed Deadline," Bloomberg, last updated June 14, 2013, accessed August 3, 2013, http://www.bloomberg.com/news/2013-06-14/ halsey-minor-asks-court-to-throw-out-dismissal-of-bankruptcy.html.

41. McCarty and Levy, "How Halsey Minor Blew Tech Fortune on Way to Bankruptcy."

42. Ibid.

43. Ibid.

44. Ibid.

45. Ibid.

46. Ibid.

47. Stephen Roth, in discussion with the author, June 2012.

48. Darrell Kong, in discussion with the author, February 2012.

49. Darrell Kong, LinkedIn profile page, accessed January 23, 2013, http://www.linkedin.com/in/ darrellkong.

50. "Seed Money Law & Legal Definition," USLegal.com, accessed August 10, 2012, http://definitions .uslegal.com/s/seed-money/.

51. Sarah E. Needleman, "'Angels' Can Fund Your Next Step," *Wall Street Journal*, last updated August 25, 2012, accessed August 29, 2012, http://online.wsj.com/news/articles/SB10000872396 3904444435045776037222242926122?mg=reno64-wsj&url=http%3A%2F%2Fonline.wsj.com% 2Farticle%2FSB10000872396390444443504577603722242926122.html.

52. "Accredited Angel Investors Defined," Merritt & Merritt & Moulton, last updated July 7, 2010, accessed July 30, 2012, http://merritt-merritt.com/vermont-law/accredited-angel-investors-defined/.

53. "VC Industry Overview," National Venture Capital Association, accessed February 8, 2013, http:// www.nvca.org/index.php?option=com_content&view=article&id=141&Itemid=589.

54. Jeffrey Sohl, "The Angel Investor Market in 2012: A Moderating Recovery Continues," Center for Venture Research, April 25, 2013; "Annual Venture Investment Dollars Decline for First Time in Three Years, according to the MoneyTree Report," National Venture Capital Association and PwC Private Equity & Venture Capital Practice, Washington, D.C., January 18, 2013.

55. David Newton, "Understanding the Financing Stages," *Entrepreneur*, last updated July 15, 2001, accessed August 10, 2012, http://www.entrepreneur.com/article/42336.

56. Nicolai Wadstrom, in discussion with the author, July 2012.

57. "Returns of Angel Investors in Groups," Kauffman Foundation, November 11, 2007, accessed February 8, 2013.

58. Ibid.

59. Jason Zasky, "Fool's Gold? Debunking the Myths of Angel Investing," *Failure Magazine*, accessed July 24, 2012, http://failuremag.com/feature/article/fools_gold/.

60. Darrell Kong, in discussion with the author, February 2012.

61. Nicolai Wadstrom, email message to author, November 27, 2013.

62. Interview with advisor, 2012. Name withheld by mutual agreement.

63. Lee Pantuso, in discussion with the author, October 2012.

64. "Peter Thiel | CrunchBase profile," CrunchBase, accessed July 26, 2012, http://www.crunchbase .com/person/peter-thiel, accessed July 26, 2012.

65. "Peter Thiel," *Forbes*, accessed July 26, 2012, http://www.forbes.com/profile/peter-thiel/.

66. David De Jong and Devon Pendleton, "Facebook IPO Makes Zuckerberg Richer Than Google Founders," Bloomberg, last updated May 18, 2012, accessed July 26, 2012, http://www.bloomberg .com/news/2012-05-17/facebook-ipo-makes-zuckerberg-richer-than-google-founders.html.

67. Laura Mandaro, "Facebook's Zuckerberg, Thiel Sell Shares," MarketWatch, last updated May 22, 2012, accessed July 26, 2012, http://articles.marketwatch.com/2012-05-22/markets/31811212_1_ peter-thiel-facebook-s-zuckerberg-facebook-insiders; Sean Ludwig, "Mark Zuckerberg owns 28.2% of Facebook, Peter Thiel has 2.5%," VentureBeat, last updated February 1, 2012, accessed July 26, 2012, http://venturebeat.com/2012/02/01/facebook-s-1-zuckerberg-ownership/; De Jong and Pendleton, "Facebook IPO Makes Zuckerberg Richer Than Google Founders."

68. Andrew Ross Sorkin, "Taking a Risk, and Hoping that Lightning Strikes Twice," *New York Times*, last updated July 23, 2012, accessed July 26, 2012, http://dealbook.nytimes.com/2012/07/23/ taking-a-risk-and-hoping-that-lightning-strikes-twice/.

69. Steve Wulf, "Err Jordan," CNN Sports Illustrated, last updated March 14, 1994, accessed September 2, 2013, http://sportsillustrated.cnn.com/basketball/nba/1999/jordan_retires/ archive/940314/.

70. "Curt Schilling Statistics and History," Baseball-Reference.com, accessed September 4, 2012, http:// www.baseball-reference.com/players/s/schilcu01.shtml#trans.

71. Jason Schwartz, "End Game: Inside the Destruction of Curt Schilling's 38 Studios," *Boston* magazine, last updated August 2012, accessed September 4, 2012, http://www.bostonmagazine .com/2012/07/38-studios-end-game/.

72. Ibid.

73. Ibid.

74. Ibid.

75. Abby Goodnough, "Trouble in Rhode Island for Boston Baseball Hero Trying Out a New Game," *New York Times*, last updated May 20, 2012, accessed September 27, 2012, http://www.nytimes.com/ 2012/05/21/us/curt-schillings-business-trouble-in-rhode-island.html.

76. Schwartz, "End Game: Inside the Destruction of Curt Schilling's 38 Studios."

77. Ibid.

78. "Curt Schilling," *Wikipedia*, accessed October 24, 2013, http://en.wikipedia.org/wiki/Curt_Schilling.

79. Schwartz, "End Game: Inside the Destruction of Curt Schilling's 38 Studios."

80. Ibid.

81. Dan Primack, "4 lessons from Curt Schilling's 38 Studios Fiasco," CNN Money, last updated June 15, 2012, accessed July 26, 2012, http://finance.fortune.cnn.com/2012/06/15/curt-schilling-38-studios/.

82. Laura Ly, "Curt Schilling's bloody sock sells for $92,613," CNN.com, last updated February 25, 2013, accessed August 31, 2013, http://edition.cnn.com/2013/02/25/sport/bloody-sock-auction.

83. "Schilling might sell bloody sock to cover loans," SI.com, last updated October 4, 2012, accessed October 4, 2013, http://sportsillustrated.cnn.com/2012/baseball/mlb/10/04/curt-schilling-bloody-sock.ap/index.html.

84. Russakow, interview.

85. Mitch Anthony, "The Retirement That Works III," *Financial Advisor Magazine* (November 2011).

86. Interview with marketing executive, 2012. Name withheld by mutual agreement.

87. Nilene R. Evans, *Frequently Asked Questions about Rule 10b5-1 Plans* (San Francisco: Morrison & Foerster LLP, 2010).

88. Ibid.

89. For illustrative purposes only. Performance data shown represents past performance. Past performance is no guarantee of future results and current performance may be higher or lower than the performance shown. Average annual total returns include reinvestment of dividends and capital gains. The principal risk in investing may include one or more of the following: market risk, foreign securities and currencies risk, and interest rate risk. Results are net of fees and expenses. Indices are not available for direct investment. Full descriptions of indices used above are located in the Sources section in this book.

Hiring an Advisor at Any Phase

1. John Bowen, email message to author, December 20, 2013.

2. John Bowen, email message to author, October 9, 2013.

3. Tim Sobolewski, "Fiduciary vs. Suitability–Which standard is best?," *FPA*, last updated September 25, 2012, accessed October 9, 2013, http://www.fpanet.org/ToolsResources/ArticlesBooksChecklists/Articles/FinancialPlanning/FiduciaryvsSuitabilityWhichstandardisbest/.

4. Interview with advisor, 2012. Name withheld by mutual agreement.

5. Interview with entrepreneur and CEO, 2012. Name withheld by mutual agreement.

6. Interview with married couple, 2011. Name withheld by mutual agreement.

7. Interview with married couple, 2012. Name withheld by mutual agreement.

8. Interview with executive, 2009. Name withheld by mutual agreement.

9. "Experience Requirement," CFP Board, accessed September 9, 2013, http://www.cfp.net/become-a-cfp-professional/cfp-certification-requirements/experience-requirement.

10. Mark P. Cussen, "CFP®, CLU or ChFC—Which Is Best?," Investopedia.com, accessed October 23, 2012, http://www.investopedia.com/articles/professionaleducation/08/cfp-clu-chfc.asp.

11. "Fiduciary Oath," NAPFA, accessed September 9, 2013, http://www.napfa.org/about/FiduciaryOath.asp.

INDEX

Made in the USA
Charleston, SC
31 December 2014